Cooking in a hurry

Cooking
in a
Hurry

by Marguerite Patten

Octopus Books

Contents

Frontispiece: HAMBURGERS

First published 1973 by Octopus Books Limited
59 Grosvenor Street, London W1

ISBN 0 7064 0251 0

© 1973 Octopus Books Limited

Some recipes and illustrations in the book were originally published
in 'Perfect Cooking' by Marguerite Patten

Produced by Mandarin Publishers Limited
14 Westlands Road, Quarry Bay, Hong Kong
and printed in Hong Kong
Typeset in Hong Kong by
Asco Trade Typesetting Ltd.

Weights and Measures

All measurements in this book are based on Imperial weights and measures.

When a cup measurement is used, this refers to a cup of 8 fl. oz. capacity.

1 Imperial pint=20 fl. oz.

Level spoon measurements are used in all the recipes.

Metric measures: for easy reference

1 kilogramme (1000 grammes)=2.2 lb
$\frac{1}{2}$ kilogramme (500 grammes)=1 lb (working equivalent)

1 litre=$1\frac{3}{4}$ pints (working equivalent)
$\frac{1}{2}$ litre=1 pint (working equivalent)

Acknowledgments

Photographs on pages 2, 11, 15, 19, 27, 31, 35, 43, 47, 61, 71, 79, 87, 91, 111 by John Lee.
Photographs on pages 49, 66, 94, 103, 107, 113, 124, 125 by Syndication International.
Photograph on page 57 by Bryce Attwell.

Introduction

It is quite wrong to suppose that good cooking needs a great deal of time spent upon it. Elaborate cooking may necessitate a lot of preparation and careful presentation of the ingredients, but if you choose the right kind of foods, you can produce a meal in a very short time.

Modern convenience foods (i.e. canned, frozen and dehydrated), as well as the excellent selection of ready cooked foods in stores and supermarkets, aid in producing a good meal within a limited space of time.

The recipes in this book are based mainly on fresh foods, for I do not want a new and inexperienced cook to imagine she must buy convenience foods in order to cook quickly. Naturally, if you substitute ready prepared, frozen or canned foods for the fresh variety you will shorten the preparation and cooking time even more than in the original recipe.

If you are in a hurry to prepare a meal these are the golden rules to remember:

1. Shop wisely, choose good quality, i.e. quick cooking foods.
2. Work methodically – put on the water for the vegetables, pre-heat the grill, light or turn on the oven etc. as soon as you get home if you need a meal quickly.

Here are some of the ways in which you may have a meal within minutes:

Meal starters: choose egg dishes, smoked fish (all ready to serve), fresh salads etc.

Soups: make use of the excellent canned and dehydrated soups and the quick suggestions on page 13.

Meats: if you wish to cook quickly then choose prime cuts of meat that may be fried or grilled.

Fish: most fish cooks quickly and you can make excellent dishes with canned tuna, canned salmon etc.

Vegetables: serve these lightly cooked or choose canned or frozen vegetables.

Desserts: the quickest and one of the best desserts is to serve fresh uncooked fruit, but the recipes in this book will enable you to prepare more elaborate desserts in a very short time. Remember cheese and biscuits with raw salads is an excellent ending to a meal – or a light meal in itself.

BEEF RISOTTO MILANAISE *(Photograph: American Rice Council)*

Ways to Save Time

Use equipment wisely:
i.e. the liquidizer (blender) saves sieving vegetables, fruits, soups, etc.
A pressure cooker can save considerable time, use for stews, soups, stocks, puddings.
Use a hand or small portable electric whisk for blending ingredients in sauces, etc., rather than a spoon.
If you have the oven in use prepare a stew for another meal, let it cook in the coolest part of the oven – reheat another day.
Prepare double quantities of pastry, etc., wrap, store half in the refrigerator or make larger quantities of prepared dishes, keep in the freezer. Your instruction book will help with ideas. Make sure you have sharp knives for quick cutting.

Use convenience foods sensibly:
Canned soups make an excellent sauce for stews and casserole dishes (choose mushroom, tomato, mixed vegetable, beef consommé, etc.)
Dehydrated (instant) potato thickens soups and stews very readily, as well as being a good vegetable.
Dehydrated (instant) onion, herbs etc. save preparing fresh foods. Onion salt, garlic salt are speedy ways of adding flavour to dishes.
Buy ready-grated cheese or grate stale cheese when time is available, store in polythene bags.
Buy ready-blanched almonds – whole, flaked or chopped.

Think ahead when menu-planning:
Often you can prepare foods for two meals, e.g. fruit or vegetable purées, pastry, etc. Always put the water on for vegetables before you shred or prepare them so it is ready for cooking. Use the minimum amount of water for cooking vegetables, this not only saves time, but retains the vitamins.

8

Meal Starters in Minutes

Fruit forms a quick start to the meal:

Avocado with crab mousse:
Blend about 4 oz. ($\frac{3}{4}$ cup) flaked canned or fresh crab with
2 tablespoons mayonnaise, 1 tablespoon lemon juice,
2 tablespoons thin cream and seasoning. Beat hard until
smooth. Halve 2 avocado pears and fill with the crab
mixture. Serve on a bed of lettuce and garnish with lemon
wedges.
Serves 4.

Melon with savoury ham rolls:
Blend $\frac{1}{4}$ pint ($\frac{2}{3}$ cup) yoghourt with 2 teaspoons horseradish
cream and 1 teaspoon made mustard. Spread over 4 slices
lean ham. Roll firmly and arrange on lettuce with several thin
slices of melon.
Serves 4.

Smoked fish are generally served with horseradish sauce,
lemon and brown bread and butter, but as they are expensive
try these quick ideas:

Salmon eggs:
Hard boil 4 eggs, remove the yolks and mash with 1 oz. butter
and seasoning, add a little lemon juice and 2 oz. neatly
chopped smoked salmon. Pile the salmon mixture back into
the white cases, top with twists of lemon and serve on lettuce.
Serves 4.
Note: Fresh or canned salmon can be used instead.

Smoked trout with devilled sauce:
Buy 2 smoked trout, remove the heads, split down the centre
and arrange each half on a bed of lettuce. Blend 2 tablespoons
thick cream with 1 tablespoon horseradish cream, 1 teaspoon
lemon juice, a good pinch curry powder, few drops Tabasco
sauce. Spread over the trout and top with slices of hard
boiled egg, cucumber and tomato.
Serves 4.
Note: Smoked mackerel can be served in the same way.

Shell fish makes delicious cocktails. The quickest cocktail
sauce is made by blending mayonnaise, lemon juice and/or
sherry and a little cream, then adding enough tomato purée
or ketchup to flavour and colour. Serve the prawns, crabmeat
or lobster on shredded lettuce and top with a generous amount
of the sauce. Chill before serving if possible.

Grapefruit Cocktails

Use canned or fresh grapefruit for the cocktails, which are
equally suitable for an hors d'oeuvre or a dessert. Lift the
segments from the liquid (if using canned fruit) or cut away
the peel from fresh fruit, divide into neat segments, discard
pips, pith and skin. Mix the grapefruit segments with other
fruits (e.g. fresh or drained canned mandarin oranges, cherries,
etc.). Sweeten if wished. Frost the edges of the glasses by
brushing with egg white and coating in sugar. Spoon the fruit
into the glasses and chill before serving.

Antipasto

*The Italian mixed hors d'oeuvre is so satisfying that it is a pity to have
small portions, so make this the substantial course of the meal.
This adaption of the classic dish can be produced with ready prepared
ingredients.*

First make up a French dressing: Blend $\frac{1}{4}$ pint ($\frac{2}{3}$ cup)
salad oil, a little made mustard, seasoning, pinch sugar and
4 tablespoons vinegar. Put into a screw topped jar; shake
hard and use as required.
Have one tray of vegetables (cooked or canned). Choose one
or more of these – green beans, artichokes, asparagus, cooked
cauliflower, broccoli, raw or cooked mushrooms, tomatoes.
Toss in a little dressing.
Next have a fish tray – tuna, salmon (canned or fresh), flaked
haddock (fresh or smoked), sardines, shell fish. Serve on
lettuce and top with a little mayonnaise.
Have interesting salads – sliced tomatoes mixed with sliced
green pepper, diced canned potatoes blended with diced
celery or celeriac, mayonnaise and chopped parsley, grated
raw carrots mixed with shredded cabbage and mayonnaise.
Arrange sliced salami, pâté, ham and garnish with a little
salad and/or fruit.
If you wish to add a 'bite' to this add small dishes of olives,
gherkins, cocktail onions, pickled cabbage or other well
flavoured ingredients.

Soups in Minutes

Where the recipe states 'stock' you can use water and stock
cubes, but when you have time to simmer bones you produce
an even better flavour. The canned beef consommé can be
used instead of a beef stock.
Onions cook much more quickly if grated, rather than
chopped, or you can use the dehydrated onions.

Beef and potato soup:

Peel and chop or grate 3 large potatoes and 1 large onion. Toss in 2 oz. ($\frac{1}{4}$ cup) margarine or butter then add $1\frac{1}{2}$ pints beef stock and seasoning. Simmer for 15 minutes then top with chopped parsley and serve.
Serves 4–6.

Greek rice and lemon soup:

Bring $1\frac{1}{2}$ pints (4 cups) chicken stock to the boil. Add 2 tablespoons long grain rice and the very finely grated rind of 1 lemon, season well. Simmer until the rice is tender. Blend the yolks of 2 eggs with the juice of the lemon in a basin. Gradually whisk in a little of the hot rice and stock mixture, then return to the pan and simmer gently, without boiling. Garnish with chopped parsley and tiny pieces of chopped green pepper.
Serves 4–6.

Tomato and prawn bisque:

Tip the contents of a 16 oz. can of tomatoes into a pan. Add $\frac{1}{4}$ pint ($\frac{2}{3}$ cup) water or chicken stock and 1–2 crushed cloves garlic. Season well and add 2 peeled diced potatoes. When these are tender stir in a little chopped parsley and approximately 4 oz. shelled prawns. Heat for a few minutes only then serve.
Serves 4–6.

Watercress cream soup:

Heat 2 oz. ($\frac{1}{4}$ cup) butter or margarine in the pan, stir in 2 oz. ($\frac{1}{2}$ cup) flour and cook for 2–3 minutes, then gradually blend in $\frac{1}{2}$ pint ($1\frac{1}{3}$ cups) chicken stock and $\frac{3}{4}$ pint (2 cups) milk. Bring to the boil, cook until thickened. Add 2–3 teaspoons lemon juice and 4 oz. chopped watercress leaves. Heat gently for a few minutes, adding seasoning.
Serves 4–6.

A Touch of Luxury

If you wish to impress guests with a classic dish make a fluffy Hollandaise sauce. This is really very speedy to prepare and delicious to eat. I think it is a splendid beginning to a meal, served over seasonal vegetables or poached or grilled fish.

Hollandaise Sauce

3 egg yolks

salt

pepper

cayenne pepper

2 tablespoons lemon juice*

3 oz. ($\frac{3}{8}$ cup) butter

*Or use white wine vinegar.

Put the egg yolks, seasoning and lemon juice into a basin over a pan of hot water or into the top of a double saucepan. Make sure the basin or alternative utensil is sufficiently large to be able to whisk well; a very narrow container hampers movement. Beat with a hand or electric whisk until the mixture is light and fluffy.

If using an electric whisk check that the egg mixture is thickening well. To do this remove from the heat, if the eggs remain thick all is well. Sometimes one can whisk so vigorously that the mixture appears to thicken, then 'flops', as it has just been aerated, not cooked as it should be. When the eggs are thick, add a small piece of butter and whisk hard until well blended. Continue like this until all the butter is incorporated. Serve hot or cold over vegetables or with fish. This is an excellent sauce for cauliflower, broccoli or asparagus.

All recipes based on this serve 6–7.

Variation:
For a richer sauce use an extra 3 oz. ($\frac{3}{8}$ cup) butter.

Egg Dishes

Dishes based on eggs are equally suitable as a starter to a meal or as a main dish. Remember that a hot egg dish should be served as soon as it is ready for it will spoil if kept waiting.
The cold stuffed eggs on page 17 are a wise choice for parties since they can be prepared well in advance.

Hot Stuffed Eggs

Hardboil the eggs, crack the shells the moment they are cooked, cool for 1 minute, then remove the shells. Halve carefully (for the eggs are very fragile when hot) and lift out the yolks. All the following quantities are enough for 4 eggs.

Cheese eggs:
Mix the yolks with 1 oz. butter or margarine, 4 oz. (1 cup) grated cheese, 1 teaspoon made mustard and seasoning. Spoon into the white cases, top with a little more cheese and heat for 1 minute under a hot grill. Serve with toast.

Devilled ham eggs:
Mix the yolks with 1 teaspoon curry powder, 1 tablespoon chutney, 2 teaspoons Worcestershire sauce and 4 oz. ham, cut into tiny pieces. Top with crisp breadcrumbs, heat for 1 minute under the grill. Serve with crusty rolls and salad.

Cheese and asparagus eggs:
Open a small can of asparagus, take off the tips to use as a garnish and put into a pan with a little cream and seasoning. Mash the rest of the asparagus with the egg yolks, seasoning and cream, put back into the white cases, top with crumbs and brown. Pour over the hot asparagus garnish. A little Parmesan cheese may be mixed with the filling or the crumbs. All of the fillings suggested on page 17 may be mixed with hot egg yolks and heated again. Always top with cheese or crumbs before heating so the filling does not dry.

16

Cold Stuffed Eggs

These can be used for a main dish with salad or as an hors d'oeuvre.
The quantities of filling are enough for 4 hard-boiled eggs. Hard-boil, cool
and shell the eggs, remove the egg yolks, mash or sieve and continue as the
suggestions below. In each case the yolks are put back into the white case.

Curried eggs (good hot as well as cold):
Blend the yolks with 2 tablespoons mayonnaise, 2–3 teaspoons
chutney and 1–2 teaspoons curry powder. Top with fine
crumbs and brown under the grill.

Anchovy eggs:
Blend the yolks with a little mayonnaise and a few drops of
anchovy essence if wished. Top with rolled anchovy fillets
or with anchovy stuffed olives.

Corn eggs:
Blend the yolks with well drained canned corn, seasoning and
a little mayonnaise (grated cheese can be added if wished).
Top with strips of fresh or canned red pepper.

Crabmeat eggs:
Blend the yolks with flaked crabmeat, using some of the dark
as well as the light flesh. Moisten with a little cream or
mayonnaise and lemon juice, season well. Top with paprika
and piped rosettes of really thick mayonnaise if desired.

Seafood eggs:
Flavour the yolks with anchovy essence and a few drops of
soy sauce if wished. Add chopped prawns or other fish if
wished, then top with shelled prawns.

Other fillings can be caviare, mashed sardines, diced ham and
tongue or flaked salmon. Always use a moist filling or
moisten with mayonnaise or a little thick cream. Season well.
Cover with foil or greaseproof paper so the eggs do not dry.

Scrambled Eggs

These are excellent for a light meal and they can be made more substantial in a variety of ways.

To make perfect scrambled egg, remember to cook the mixture slowly and to be generous with the amount of butter or margarine. Allow 2 eggs per person (more if very hungry). Break the eggs, add seasoning and beat – do not over-beat. Add 1–2 tablespoons milk or cream if wished; this makes a lighter scrambled egg, but if omitted you have a richer mixture. Heat at least $\frac{1}{2}$ oz. (1 teaspoon) butter or margarine for 2 eggs – more if possible – in a saucepan or frying pan and turn the heat low. Add the eggs and stir a little as they begin to set – over-stirring is a mistake. Serve as soon as lightly set.

Add diced chicken, ham, chopped shell fish or flaked fish or grated cheese to the eggs. Make sure the pieces are small so they heat through or heat these first in the butter or margarine and milk or cream, then add the eggs.

Pipérade

1–2 oz. butter or use half butter and half olive oil	1–2 onions
	1–2 tomatoes
1 green pepper	1 clove garlic
1 red pepper – (or use half a green and half a red pepper)	6 eggs
	seasoning

Heat the butter, or butter and oil, in a pan. Add the prepared peppers, either diced or cut into thin rings (discard the seeds and core), the peeled sliced or chopped onions and tomatoes and the crushed clove of garlic. Cook gently until tender, then add the beaten seasoned eggs and scramble until lightly set.

Serve with crusty French bread or with crisp toast.

Serves 2–3 as a main dish or 6 as a light hors d'oeuvre.

Baked Eggs

$\frac{1}{2}$–1 oz. butter   2 eggs
   or margarine   seasoning

Put half the butter or margarine into one or two containers
(use one container for a main dish, two for hors d'oeuvre).
Heat the butter or margarine for a few minutes in a moderate
to moderately hot oven, 375–400°F, Gas Mark 5–6. Break the
eggs over the hot butter or margarine, add a little seasoning,
then the rest of the fat in one or two small knobs. Bake for
just over 10 minutes towards the top of the oven. Serve with
a teaspoon, while still very hot.
Serves 2 as an hors d'oeuvre or 1 as a main meal.

Variations:
Put grated, cottage or cream cheese into the dish or dishes,
with the butter or margarine. Heat this for a few minutes,
then add the egg or eggs, seasoning, more grated (not cream
or cottage) cheese and butter or margarine. Cook as above.
Put a layer of thin or thick cream over the hot butter or
margarine, then add the egg or eggs, seasoning, another layer
of cream and the remaining butter or margarine. Cook as above.
Add chopped ham, chicken, prawns or asparagus tips to the
butter or margarine, heat, then add the egg or eggs,
seasoning and the rest of the butter or margarine. Cook as
above. All these variations make excellent light dishes.

Swiss Omelette

1 oz. butter   seasoning
4 eggs   3 oz. ($\frac{3}{4}$ cup) grated Gruyére cheese

Grease a shallow dish with half the butter, melt the
remainder. Beat the eggs lightly with seasoning. Put half the
cheese over the butter, then the beaten eggs, then the rest of
the cheese and melted butter. Bake as above.
Serves 2.

Eggs Mornay

4 eggs
1 oz. butter or margarine
1 oz. flour

$\frac{1}{2}$ pint ($1\frac{1}{3}$ cups) milk
seasoning
4 oz. (1 cup) grated Cheddar
   cheese

Boil the eggs; these can be firmly set or hard-boiled. Plunge
into cold water to cool, then remove the shells.
Heat the butter or margarine in a pan, stir in the flour and
cook for several minutes. Gradually blend in the milk and
bring to the boil, then cook until the sauce has thickened.
Season well, stir in the grated cheese. Do not continue
cooking after the cheese has melted. Arrange the whole or
halved eggs in a dish, top with the cheese sauce and serve.
Serves 4 as an hors d'oeuvre or 2 as a main dish.

Fried Eggs Plus

Fried eggs are cooked in minutes and can form a complete
meal by themselves or with fried or grilled bacon, sausages
etc. Heat the fat – this can be bacon fat, butter or cooking
fat. Pour in the eggs and cook quickly.

Fried Eggs Turque

4–6 chickens' livers
2 oz. ($\frac{1}{4}$ cup) butter
$\frac{1}{2}$ tablespoon chopped parsley

4 large tomatoes
seasoning
4 eggs
French bread

Slice the chickens' livers and fry in half the hot butter until
tender. Add the chopped parsley and arrange in the centre of
a hot dish. While the livers are cooking, heat the skinned
chopped tomatoes with seasoning until a thick purée. Spoon
over the livers. Fry the eggs in the remaining hot butter and
arrange round the tomato and liver mixture.
Serves 4.

Making Omelettes

To make a perfect omelette is a great achievement – if over-cooked it is dry and unappetizing, but if light and moist it is a most delicious dish.

To make a plain omelette:
Use the proportion of ingredients as on page 25, but do not separate the eggs. Heat the butter in the pan, do not let this discolour, but make sure it is sufficiently hot to set the eggs the moment they go into the pan. When the eggs are poured into the pan wait about 30 seconds, until a thin layer is set at the base, then tilt the pan, at the same time loosening the mixture from round the edges, so the top liquid egg flows underneath – this is known as 'working' the omelette. Cook until set, add any filling (see below and page 23) then fold or roll away from the handle and serve.

Store cupboard omelette:
Ingredients as Plain Omelette *plus* can asparagus spears, can potatoes, little extra butter, 1–2 oz. diced Cheddar cheese, parsley.
Chop the asparagus stalks, reserving the tips for garnish. Fry the drained diced potatoes in extra butter until golden. Mix the asparagus, potato and cheese. Cook as the Plain Omelette, adding the potato mixture while the egg is still soft. Fold and serve garnished with hot asparagus tips and parsley.

Cheese omelette:
Ingredients as Plain Omelette *plus* 1–2 oz. ($\frac{1}{4}$–$\frac{1}{2}$ cup) grated cheese. Cook as the Plain Omelette but add the cheese just before it is completely set. Fold or roll and serve as the Plain Omelette. Garnish with grated cheese and parsley.

Ham omelette:
Ingredients as Plain Omelette *plus* 2 oz. ($\frac{1}{4}$ cup) diced cooked ham. Mix the ham with the beaten eggs. Cook as the Plain Omelette.

22   STORE CUPBOARD OMELETTE *(Photograph: John West Foods Ltd.)*

Mushroom omelette:

Ingredients as Plain Omelette *plus* 1–2 oz. ($\frac{1}{4}$–$\frac{1}{2}$ cup) chopped fresh mushrooms and a little extra butter.
Cook the mushrooms in some of the butter. Mix with the beaten eggs. Cook as the Plain Omelette. Garnish with more mushrooms or parsley.

Prawn omelette:

Ingredients as Plain Omelette *plus* 2 oz. ($\frac{1}{4}$ cup) chopped shelled prawns. Mix the prawns with the beaten eggs. Cook as the Plain Omelette. Garnish with a thick slice of lemon.

Potato omelette:

Blend about 2 oz. ($\frac{1}{4}$ cup) very smooth mashed potatoes with each mixture of 2 eggs and cook as the Soufflé Omelette.

Omelette aux fines herbes:

Ingredients as Plain Omelette *plus* 1–2 teaspoons freshly chopped herbs or $\frac{1}{4}$–$\frac{1}{2}$ teaspoon dried herbs. Mix the herbs with the beaten eggs. Cook and serve as the Plain Omelette. Garnish with freshly chopped herbs.

Bacon filled omelette:

Ingredients as Plain Omelette *plus* 2 rashers of bacon and 1 tomato. Chop and fry the bacon, keep hot. Cook as the Plain Omelette, add the bacon then fold or roll. Serve as the Plain Omelette, garnished with cooked or raw tomato slices.

To save time:

If you make omelettes very regularly then prepare small containers of filling and freeze these – label carefully – they will then enable you to make an omelette in minutes.

Economy hint:

Fry a little diced bread in the butter before adding the eggs, etc., this makes a very substantial omelette, or fry diced cooked potatoes or other vegetables.

Soufflé Omelette

2 or 3 eggs
seasoning or 1 teaspoon sugar
  for a sweet omelette
1 tablespoon water

1 oz. butter
filling or flavouring
  (see individual recipes)

Separate the yolks from the whites. Beat the yolks with seasoning or sugar, and water. Whisk the egg whites until very stiff, fold into the yolks. Heat the butter in the pan. Switch on the grill.

Pour the fluffy egg mixture into the hot butter. Allow to set and 'work as page 22. You will find this more difficult as the mixture is less liquid. When the omelette is about half-cooked, put the pan under the grill (with the heat to medium) and complete the cooking.

Add any filling required. This thicker omelette is more difficult to fold (you cannot roll it) so make a shallow cut across the centre, then fold. Slide or tip on to the hot serving dish or plate.

All recipes based on this serve 1 as a main dish or 2 as a light hors d'oeuvre or dessert.

Sweet Fillings for Omelettes

Nut omelette:
Follow the Soufflé Omelette recipe and blend 1–2 tablespoons chopped blanched almonds, hazel, pecan or walnuts with the egg yolks. Fill with hot sweetened apricot purée or jam.

Fruit omelette:
Use thin cream instead of the water in the Soufflé Omelette. Fill with hot fruit purée or sliced uncooked sweetened fresh fruit. The fruit can be flavoured with brandy or liqueur.

Jam omelette:
Make the omelette as the Soufflé Omelette and fill with hot jam or jelly. A delicious omelette is made by adding finely grated orange or lemon rind to the egg yolks then filling with hot marmalade.

Fish Dishes

The quickest methods of cooking fish are grilling and frying, for the fish can be cooked with little, if any, preparation and served immediately without a sauce, or with a very quick sauce.

Fish meunière:
Do not coat the fish for this method of frying. Choose fillets of white fish (sole, whiting, plaice) or trout. For 4 large or 8 smaller fillets use at least 3 oz. ($\frac{3}{8}$ cup) butter. Season the fish lightly, fry in the butter until tender. Lift out of the pan and keep hot: check you have sufficient butter to pour over the fish when it is browned, if not add more. Heat until golden brown, add 1 tablespoon lemon juice, 1 tablespoon chopped parsley and 1–2 teaspoons capers. Heat and spoon over the fish.
Serves 4.

Fish gratinée:
Fry as above, but be a little more sparing with the butter. Lift the hot fish on to a flame-proof dish, spoon over any butter left, top with grated cheese and breadcrumbs. Heat under a hot grill until brown.
Serves 4.

Fish and bacon whirls:
Choose coated frozen fish or coat fairly small fillets of plaice or whiting (this makes it easier to put on the bacon) with beaten egg and breadcrumbs. Fry in a little hot oil, butter or fat until crisp and brown, but not quite cooked. Lift out on to a plate. Take rashers of streaky bacon and cut into long thin strips. Twist round the fish, secure with a wooden cocktail stick if necessary and return to the frying pan for a few minutes. Add halved or sliced tomatoes and cook with the bacon and fish.

Grilled fish with soured cream sauce:
Put 4 well seasoned fish cutlets (cod, fresh haddock, hake are
very suitable) into a flame-proof dish, top with a little
seasoning and a squeeze of lemon juice. Add small pieces of
butter or margarine and cook for the same time. Blend $\frac{1}{4}$ pint
($\frac{2}{3}$ cup) dairy soured cream (or thin cream plus about 1
tablespoon lemon juice) with 2 teaspoons capers, 2 teaspoons
chopped gherkins. Spoon over the fish. Lower the heat and
cook gently for a further 6–7 minutes.
Serves 4.

Creamed Tuna à la King

$\frac{1}{4}$ pint ($\frac{2}{3}$ cup) mayonnaise
4 tablespoons top of the milk or
    thin cream
small can sweet corn

1 green pepper
seasoning
medium can tuna fish
1 tablespoon chopped parsley

Put the mayonnaise, milk or cream and well drained sweet
corn into a basin over a pan of boiling water or into the top of
a double saucepan. Heat steadily. Meanwhile dice the green
pepper (discard core and seeds) and cook for a few minutes
in well seasoned water, drain, add to the mayonnaise mixture.
Finally add the flaked tuna fish, plus any liquid from the can
and the parsley. Heat for a few minutes and serve with
vegetables or toast.
Serves 4.

Variation:
Use salmon or cooked white fish instead of tuna.

Sole with White Wine Sauce

4 large or 8 smaller fillets of sole
    (or use other white fish, whiting
    is excellent for this dish)
seasoning
about 2 oz. ($\frac{1}{4}$ cup) butter
about $\frac{2}{3}$ pint (nearly 2 cups)
    white wine

1 oz. ($\frac{1}{4}$ cup) flour
$\frac{1}{4}$ pint ($\frac{2}{3}$ cup) milk
2–3 tablespoons thick or thin
    cream
Garnish:
paprika
1 lemon

Roll or fold the fillets of fish, put into a baking dish and season lightly. Top with nearly half the butter and white wine. Cover the dish and bake in a moderate oven, 350–375°F, Gas Mark 4–5, for about 20 minutes or a little less, since the fish has to be kept waiting while finishing the sauce. Meanwhile heat the remainder of the butter in a saucepan, stir in the flour and continue stirring over a low heat for a few minutes. Gradually blend in the milk and bring to the boil, stirring until very thick. Lift the fish on to a very hot serving dish, strain the liquid from cooking the fish gradually into the thick sauce, then stir gently until smooth. Stir in the cream, heat without boiling. Pour over the baked fish, top with paprika and garnish with sliced lemon.
Serves 4.

Variations:
Sole véronique: Add a few de-seeded grapes (peeled if wished) to the wine and fish. Garnish with more grapes and lemon.
Sole Sevilla: Place slices of orange under each rolled fillet when cooked and proceed as the recipe above. Garnish with de-seeded grapes; peeled if wished.

Savoury Grilled Turbot

3 oz. ($\frac{3}{8}$ cup) butter
1 tablespoon lemon juice
$\frac{1}{2}$–1 teaspoon paprika
seasoning

4 steaks turbot or other white fish
Garnish:
parsley, lemon

Heat the butter in a pan until it turns golden brown. This gives a delicious flavour to the fish, but it is essential the butter does not become too dark. Add the lemon juice, paprika and seasoning. Brush one side of the fish with some of the butter mixture and put on the greased grid or on buttered foil. Cook under the heated grill until just tender (do not over-cook), turning once.
Serve topped with any hot butter and garnish with parsley and lemon. Serve with new potatoes.
Serves 4.

Meat Dishes

The young prime tender pieces of meat are those to choose for quick cooking, i.e. steaks, chops and cutlets of pork, veal and lamb, together with lean gammon or ham.
For even speedier meals you can buy ready cooked meats in good grocers' shops or supermarkets and turn these into interesting dishes. If you intend heating cooked ham, etc., then ask for the slices to be cut fairly thick, for thin slices dry and become very tasteless.
An economy meat that cooks quite quickly is minced beef.

To Grill Steaks and Chops, etc.

Less fat is needed when grilling meats than frying, but if you require lean meat to be richly moist then be fairly generous.
To save time and to ensure moist meat: Pre-heat the grill, so the outside of the meat is sealed quickly.
The butter or other fat can be spread over the lean meat, but a more even distribution is given if this is melted first, or if you use oil, and the meat brushed with the melted fat before and during cooking. This enables other flavours to be added to the fat and these impregnate the meat during cooking; for a more definite flavour marinate the meat before cooking.
Grill the meat quickly on either side, then lower the heat and/or move the grill pan further away from the heat of the grill. To save using another cooking utensil cook tomatoes, mushrooms and onion rings at the same time as the meat. Melt a little fat in the grill pan, put in the vegetables, season well and cook for a few minutes, turning if necessary, under the grill. Put the meat on the grid above this and continue cooking. Heat fruit round the meat as you grill; cooked well drained prunes are excellent with beef or pork, pineapple rings, peaches, apricots, apple rings blend with lamb or pork. Baste well with melted butter, oil or other fat.

30

To Fry Steaks and Chops, etc.

You will need a generous amount of butter, fat or dripping when you fry lean beef steaks – choose rump, fillet, sirloin or other tender cuts. Heat the butter or alternative fat and fry the steak rapidly on either side for 2–3 minutes to seal in the juices, then lower the heat and cook to personal taste. Chops of pork or lamb need little if any butter or other fat, but veal chops and cutlets and very lean lamb need a little butter or other fat. Below are ways to make more original dishes with fried meat.

Lamb cutlets with cucumber sauce:
Fry 8 small lamb cutlets. Meanwhile peel and dice $\frac{1}{2}$ small cucumber and simmer for 5 minutes in salted water, drain well. Lift the meat from the pan, stir in 2 teaspoons flour, $\frac{1}{2}$ pint ($1\frac{1}{3}$ cup) yoghourt, a good shake pepper and salt, the cucumber and a little chopped chives and chopped parsley. Simmer for a few minutes only (the cucumber is nicer if not too soft), stirring all the time, then spoon over the cutlets and serve. This is equally good with veal or very lean pork.
Serves 4.

Pork chops with apples in mustard sauce:
Fry 4 pork chops then remove from the pan and keep hot. Pour away all the fat except 2 tablespoons. Peel and slice 2 or 3 dessert apples and cook in the hot fat for about 5 minutes, turning once or twice. Lift out and arrange round the pork. Blend 1 tablespoon made mustard, 2 teaspoons flour, 2 tablespoons tomato ketchup and $\frac{1}{4}$ pint ($\frac{2}{3}$ cup) thin cream or top of the milk with the fat remaining in the pan. Season well and stir for about 5 minutes over a gentle heat, until a smooth thickened mixture. Spoon over the chops.
Serves 4.

Spiced steak: Cut about 1 lb. sirloin or other good quality steak into strips. Slice 2 onions and fry in 1 oz. butter, then

add another 1 oz. butter to the pan and fry the steak for 2–3 minutes only. Blend 1 tablespoon flour, 2 teaspoons curry powder and a shake cayenne pepper with just *under* $\frac{1}{2}$ pint ($1\frac{1}{4}$ cups) stock, add 2 teaspoons soy sauce, 1 teaspoon Worcestershire sauce. Pour over the onions and steak and cook until the steak is tender and the sauce very hot. Serve with cooked rice.
Serves 4.

To save continual grilling and frying try cooking meat in foil parcels – the following recipe is delicious and you have all the meal, meat and vegetables, cooked together with no cooking utensils to clean.

Parcelled Veal

2 oz. ($\frac{1}{4}$ cup) butter or bacon fat	1 large onion
4 cutlets, chops or fillets of veal	4 large tomatoes
seasoning	4 tablespoons sherry or stock

Cut 4 squares of heavy foil (or use a double thickness). Spread half the softened butter or bacon fat over the centre of the foil. Put the meat on this, season lightly, then add very thin slices of onion, thick slices of tomato and the sherry or stock. Season again, and top with the rest of the butter or bacon fat.
Fold the foil to make neat parcels, put these into a roasting tin, it makes them easier to remove, and cook above the centre of a hot oven, 425–450°F, Gas Mark 6–7, for 35–40 minutes. Unwrap the parcels carefully and tip on to the serving plates.
Serves 4.

Kidney Kebabs with Orange Sauce

Sauce:
2 oranges
$\frac{1}{2}$ pint ($1\frac{1}{3}$ cups) brown stock
1 oz. cornflour
1 oz. butter
seasoning
$\frac{1}{2}$ – 1 teaspoon sugar
To serve:
boiled rice

Kebabs:
8–12 skinned whole or halved
  lambs' kidneys
seasoning
pinch mixed dried herbs
about 12 mushrooms
12 small cocktail onions
4 rashers bacon
2 oz. ($\frac{1}{4}$ cup) melted butter

Pare the rind very thinly from the oranges and simmer this
in half the stock for about 5 minutes. Strain, return to the pan.
Blend the cornflour with the rest of the stock, add to the
liquid in the pan with the juice of the oranges, the butter,
seasoning and sugar. Bring to the boil, cook gently and stir
until smooth and thickened.

Meanwhile, roll the kidneys in seasoning and herbs, put on to
4 metal skewers with the mushrooms, onions and halved
bacon rashers in neat rolls. Brush with the melted butter and
cook under a hot grill for about 8 minutes. Turn several
times during cooking, so the food cooks evenly. Serve on a
bed of boiled rice with the orange sauce.

Serves 4.

Note: extra orange segments can be added to the sauce, if
liked.

Variations:
The kidneys may be placed on well buttered foil on the pan
and cooked with the other ingredients under the grill.
Kidneys in Pork wine sauce: Cook the kidneys as above or
fry or grill in butter. Omit the oranges and add 4 tablespoons
port wine instead.

Beef Creole

4 minute (very thin) steaks
salt, black pepper
Tabasco sauce
1 onion

3 oz. ($\frac{3}{8}$ cup) butter or margarine
1 green pepper
$\frac{1}{4}$ pint ($\frac{2}{3}$ cup) stock

Flatten the steaks with a rolling pin, season with a little salt, a generous amount of pepper and a few drops Tabasco sauce. Chop the onion finely, fry for 2 minutes only in the hot butter or margarine. Add the steaks and diced pepper (discard core and seeds), fry for 2 minutes. Add the stock, bring to the boil. Serve at once with rice.
Serves 4.

Steak au Malaga

1 can stewed steak
$\frac{1}{4}$ pint ($\frac{2}{3}$ cup) Marsala wine
   (or other red wine)

about 12 tiny cocktail onions
few olives

Heat the steak with the wine and onions. Garnish with the olives just before serving.
Serves 3–4.

Steak Charlotte

4 large slices bread
2 oz. ($\frac{1}{4}$ cup) margarine or fat

1 can stewed steak
chopped parsley
1 green pepper

Cut the bread into neat fingers and fry in the hot margarine or fat until crisp and golden brown on both sides. Put half at the bottom of a shallow oven-proof dish. Mix the steak with parsley and diced green pepper (discard core and seeds). Put into the dish then top with the remainder of the fried fingers of bread and heat for about 30 minutes in the centre of a very moderate to moderate oven, 350–375°F, Gas Mark 4–5.
Serves 4.

Barbecued Lamb:
Crush 1–2 cloves garlic very finely (or use a generous amount of ready-prepared garlic or garlic salt). Blend with
2 tablespoons oil or melted fat, 2 tablespoons red wine,
1 tablespoon concentrated tomato purée, 1 teaspoon
Worcestershire sauce, 2 teaspoons chopped fresh mint (or a good pinch dried mint), a generous shake of pepper and
1 teaspoon brown sugar. Pour into a shallow dish. Put 4 good sized lamb chops or 8 cutlets in this mixture, leave for $\frac{1}{2}$ hour, turn and leave for another $\frac{1}{2}$ hour. No fat or other flavouring is needed during cooking.
Note: Veal or pork could be prepared in the same way.
Serves 4.

Steak au Poivre

4 fillet or other good quality   salt
   steaks   2 oz. ($\frac{1}{4}$ cup) butter
few peppercorns

Put the steak on a flat surface. Crush the peppercorns with a rolling pin and press on to either side of the steak. Add a light dusting of salt. Heat the butter in the pan and fry the steaks as instructions on page 32.

Variations:
The above recipe is the simplest form of presenting this dish. If a more elaborate one is required proceed as above until the steaks are just cooked. Lift out of the pan on to a hot dish and add approximately $\frac{1}{4}$ pint ($\frac{2}{3}$ cup) thick cream and heat in the frying pan, stirring well to absorb the meat juices. Add a little extra seasoning if wished, but remember the steaks will be very peppery. Lastly, stir in 1–2 tablespoons of brandy. Pour the sauce over the steaks and serve. A little chopped parsley, or chopped chives, may be added to the cream sauce.
Serves 4.

Ways of Cooking Liver

When you wish to cook liver quickly choose calf's or lamb's liver or pig's liver. The latter is not as delicate in flavour, so needs fairly 'robust' ingredients cooked with it. Never over-cook liver, for it makes it both dry and tough. Serve as soon as possible after cooking.

Liver Normandy

1 lb. lamb's or pig's liver
1 oz. flour
3 oz. ($\frac{3}{8}$ cup) butter
1 large onion
To serve:
cooked rice or creamed potato

$\frac{1}{2}$ pint ($1\frac{1}{3}$ cups) dry cider
seasoning
2 dessert apples
Garnish:
black and green olives

Cut the liver into fingers, coat with the flour and seasoning. Heat half the butter in the pan and fry the liver for a few minutes only, put on one side. Heat the rest of the butter and fry rings of apple (cored but not peeled) and thinly sliced onion until golden coloured. Add the cider and simmer until the apple and onion are tender. Replace the liver and heat through. Serve in a border of cooked rice or creamed potato (dehydrated potato is very quick and ideal for this purpose). Garnish with a few black and green olives.
Serves 4.

Variations:
Creamed liver: Use the method of cooking above, but omit the apples. Use only $\frac{1}{4}$ pint ($\frac{2}{3}$ cup) cider or white wine and blend in $\frac{1}{4}$ pint ($\frac{2}{3}$ cup) thin cream just before serving.
Paprika liver: Use sliced tomatoes instead of apples. Blend 1–2 teaspoons paprika with the flour and seasoning. Use either cider as the basic recipe or white wine or stock. Serve with cooked noodles.

38   LIVER NORMANDY *(Photograph: Fruit Producers Council)*

Wiener Schnitzel

These are delicious escallops of veal or pork.

4 fillets veal or pork
seasoning
1 tablespoon flour
1 egg
1 lemon

3–4 tablespoons fine soft
 breadcrumbs
4 oz. ($\frac{1}{2}$ cup) fat or butter* for
 frying
little chopped parsley

*If using butter add a small amount of frying oil so the butter does
not darken.

The meat must be very thin, so flatten with a rolling pin if
necessary. Coat the slices of meat in seasoned flour, then
beaten egg and breadcrumbs. Heat the fat or butter and oil in
the pan. Add the meat and cook quickly on one side, turn
with tongs or two knives (do not pierce with the prongs of a
fork as this allows the meat juices to escape). Fry quickly on
the second side, lower the heat and continue cooking for a
total time of about 10 minutes only.
Garnish with slices of lemon and chopped parsley. If the lemon
and parsley are put on the meat *in* the pan and warmed for
1–2 minutes, the maximum flavour can be extracted. For a
more elaborate garnish top the lemon slices with chopped
hard-boiled eggs, capers and anchovy fillets.
Serves 4.

Variations:
If you buy very small pieces of veal and serve 2–3 per person
the cooking time is even shorter than the time taken in the
above recipe.
Veal in paprika sauce: Do not coat the veal, fry in butter as
instructions above. Remove the veal when tender. Blend
2 teaspoons paprika (a sweet, not hot flavouring) with a shake
of cayenne pepper and $\frac{1}{4}$ pint ($\frac{2}{3}$ cup) thin cream and stir into
the pan, absorbing all the meat juice. A very little dry sherry
can also be added. Heat gently, pour over the veal.

Lamb and Raisin Patties

1 lb. uncooked lean lamb
(preferably cut from the leg)
1 oz. butter, oil or dripping from
lamb
1 oz. ($\frac{1}{4}$ cup) flour
$\frac{1}{4}$ pint ($\frac{2}{3}$ cup) brown stock
3 oz. ($\frac{1}{2}$ cup) raisins

1 tablespoon chopped parsley
seasoning
Coating:
1 egg
2–3 oz. crisp breadcrumbs
oil or fat for frying

Mince the lamb. Heat the butter, oil or dripping then stir in
the flour and cook for 2 or 3 minutes. Gradually blend in the
stock. Bring to the boil, add the raisins, then stir until
thickened (by adding the raisins at this stage you make them
more moist). Stir in the parsley and lamb, then season well.
Allow the mixture to cool. As this is rather soft form into
8 small cakes and chill well before coating. Coat in beaten egg
and crumbs then fry in hot oil or fat until crisp and golden
brown on both sides. Lower the heat and fry steadily for
another 5–6 minutes to make sure the lamb is thoroughly
cooked.
Serves 4.
Variations:
To make a firmer textured patty add 2 oz. soft breadcrumbs to
the mixture.
Omit the raisins and add chopped chutney instead (this is very
moist so be a little sparing with the stock or use the version
including breadcrumbs).
To use cooked meat:
Use minced cooked lamb, but since this loses a little of the
moist texture, add a small proportion of fat as well as using
the lean. You can use the basic recipe or the variation above
that includes breadcrumbs.
Savoury lamb patties:
Increase the amount of butter or oil to 2 oz. ($\frac{1}{4}$ cup) and fry a
chopped onion and 1–2 crushed cloves garlic before
proceeding with the recipe.

Speedy Moussaka

2 onions
3 oz. ($\frac{3}{8}$ cup) fat
1 oz. ($\frac{1}{4}$ cup) flour
$\frac{1}{2}$ pint (1$\frac{1}{2}$ cup) stock or water
  and 1 stock cube
1 lb. minced beef (or other raw
  minced meat – lamb is
  excellent).

seasoning
good pinch mixed herbs
12 oz. peeled potatoes
1 aubergine
$\frac{1}{2}$ pint (1$\frac{1}{3}$ cups) full cream
  evaporated milk
6 oz. (1$\frac{1}{2}$ cups) grated cheese

Peel and chop the onions, toss in half the fat for a few minutes, then add the flour and cook for 2 or 3 minutes. Gradually blend in the stock or water and stock cube, bring to the boil and cook until thickened. Add the meat, stir very well to break up the lumps that form. Season, add the herbs, then bring the mixture to the boil, stir again. Lower the heat, cover the pan, allow to simmer for 35–40 minutes. Stir once or twice during the cooking, as the mixture is very thick. Meanwhile boil the potatoes in salted water, drain and slice fairly thickly. Slice the unpeeled aubergine thinly and toss in the remaining fat until tender. Put half the potatoes and half the sliced aubergine into a casserole, top with a third of the evaporated milk and cheese and seasoning. Add the meat mixture, another third of the milk and cheese and seasoning, then the rest of the aubergine and potato slices. Pour the remainder of the milk over the top very carefully, sprinkle with the last of the cheese. Season the mixture and bake for 30 minutes in the centre of a moderate oven, 350–375°F, Gas Mark 4–5.

Serves 4–6.

Variations:

Make a cheese sauce with 1 oz. ($\frac{1}{4}$ cup) flour, 1 oz. margarine, $\frac{3}{4}$ pint (2 cups) milk, seasoning and 4–6 oz. (1–1$\frac{1}{2}$ cups) grated cheese. Use instead of the evaporated milk and cheese. Add an egg to the evaporated milk or the cheese sauce.

To save time:

Use canned stewing steak and omit the first stage. Mix the stewing steak with 1–2 tablespoons dehydrated onion and allow it to stand for 30 minutes to improve the flavour.

Bobotee

1 large onion
2–3 large tomatoes
2 oz. ($\frac{1}{4}$ cup) fat
1–1$\frac{1}{4}$ lb. minced meat
  (preferably lamb)
$\frac{1}{4}$ pint ($\frac{2}{3}$ cup) stock

2–3 tablespoons flaked blanched
  almonds (optional)
seasoning
2 eggs
$\frac{1}{2}$ pint (1$\frac{1}{3}$ cups) milk

Peel and grate the onion (or use dehydrated onion), skin and slice the tomatoes and toss in the heated fat for a few minutes. Mix with the minced meat and stock and simmer for about 25 minutes, stirring several times to keep the mixture smooth. Add the almonds and seasoning and put into a shallow oven-proof casserole.
Beat the eggs with seasoning, add the milk. Pour over the meat mixture and bake for about 45 minutes in the centre of a very moderate to moderate oven, 350–375°F, Gas Mark 4–5. Cover the dish during baking if you want a soft topping or leave the dish uncovered for a firmer custard 'crust'.
Serves 4–5.

Variations:
Add more almonds to the custard mixture.
Sprinkle a thick layer of grated cheese over the egg and milk mixture before baking.
Soufflé topped Bobotee: Prepare the dish as the recipe above, but make the custard mixture with 1 egg, 1 egg yolk, seasoning and milk only. Bake for about 35 minutes. Take a third egg and separate the yolk and the white, add this white to the one left from the custard mixture. Beat the yolk with seasoning, 2 tablespoons thick cream and 2 tablespoons finely grated cheese. Whisk the egg whites until stiff, fold into the egg yolk and cheese mixture. Pile over the top of the custard, add a few flaked almonds. Return to the oven for 10 minutes.

Hasty Hamburgers

1 lb. minced beef (choose rump, sirloin or other prime steak for tenderness, chuck steak for economy)
seasoning
1 egg yolk (optional)
pinch mixed herbs
2–3 teaspoons oil (optional)
1 large onion
1 tablespoon seasoned flour
1–2 oz. fat for frying

Mix the beef, seasoning, egg yolk and herbs together. If wished omit the egg yolk. If the meat is very lean add the oil. Form into 4 round flat cakes. Peel and cut the onion into rings, then coat in seasoned flour. Fry the onion rings in the fat and keep hot, then add the meat cakes and cook on both sides. Lower the heat and continue cooking for 2–6 minutes according to personal taste and type of meat used (chuck steak naturally takes longer). Serve with vegetables or on toasted halved hamburger rolls.
Serves 4.

Variations:
Hamburger Indienne: Ingredients as above but add 1–2 teaspoons curry powder with the seasoning, together with a little finely grated onion; onion rings. Cook as the basic Hamburger. Top with rings of fried pineapple and chutney.
Hamburger plus cheese: Ingredients as above, plus 4 slices Cheddar or processed cheese. Cook the onion rings and hamburgers. Put the hamburgers on top of halved toasted rolls, cover with the cheese and brown under the grill. Top with the onion rings. If preferred, omit the fresh onion and top with rings of tomato and several small pickled onions.
Nutty Hamburger: Ingredients as above, plus 2–3 tablespoons salted peanuts. Cook as the basic Hamburger, top with peanuts before serving. A few chopped nuts may also be added to the Hamburger mixture.
Pimento Hamburger: Ingredients as above, plus sliced rings of red and/or green pepper. Cook as the basic Hamburger and top with rings of fried pepper.

Gammon with Pineapple and Corn Sauce

4 small or 2 larger slices of lean
   gammon
about 2 oz. (about $\frac{1}{4}$ cup) butter
3–4 rings of canned pineapple
2 tablespoons syrup from
   the can of pineapple
Garnish:
watercress

1 oz. flour
$\frac{1}{2}$ pint ($1\frac{1}{3}$ cups) milk
seasoning
3–4 tablespoons cooked
sweet corn
2–3 teaspoons chopped parsley
Sauce:
1 onion
1 oz. butter

If you like very crisp fat on grilled gammon remove the rind.
If you prefer the fat to be fairly soft then leave the rind on.
In either case snip the edges of the gammon, this prevents it
from curling. Never pre-heat the grill when cooking gammon,
for if too hot it encourages the edges of the gammon to curl
and burn. Brush the gammon with melted butter and cook for
several minutes on the one side, turn, brush with more butter
and continue cooking.

When the gammon is nearly ready add the halved well
drained rings of pineapple to the grill pan. Brush these with
the remainder of the butter and heat thoroughly.

Make the sauce while the gammon is cooking. Chop the onion
very finely. Heat the butter in a pan, stir in the flour and
cook for several minutes.

Gradually blend in the milk, add the onion. Bring to the boil
and cook until thickened, stirring all the time. Season the
sauce, add the sweet corn and parsley and keep warm until
ready to serve.

Place the gammon and pineapple on a plate and garnish with
watercress.

At the last minute whisk the pineapple syrup into the sauce,
and serve the sauce as accompaniment to the gammon.

Normandy Pork

5 or 6 loin or chump pork chops
  (or thick slices pork)
2–3 onions
½ pint (1⅓ cups) white wine
1 tablespoon Calvados (optional)

pinch fresh or dried sage
2–3 dessert apples
seasoning
little olive oil

Fry the chops in a large pan for about 5–8 minutes until
lightly browned. Lift out of the pan. Peel and chop the onions
and toss in any fat left in the pan until tender but not brown.
Add the wine, Calvados, sage, peeled and chopped apples and
seasoning. Spoon into a large shallow casserole. Arrange the
chops on top. Try to keep the skin above the wine so it
crisps, as in the picture, and brush this with the oil. Do not
cover the dish. Cook for 40–45 minutes in the centre of a
moderate oven, 350–375°F, Gas Mark 4–5.
Serves 5–6.

Variations:
Pork in cider: Omit the white wine and Calvados and use
cider instead. A sweet cider is particularly good.
Pork véronique: Fry the chops as above. Chop 1 onion only,
toss in the hot fat, add just the ½ pint (1⅓ cups) white wine.
Omit the sage and add a few skinned de-seeded grapes and
seasoning. Cook as basic recipe. Lift the chops on to a hot
dish when ready. Pour the liquid and grapes into a pan, stir in
3 tablespoons thick cream, heat gently. Season if required and
spoon over the chops. Garnish with fresh grapes.

To save cooking time:
The chops may be fried and the sauce in the basic recipe
prepared in a separate pan. This means you must use a little
butter or spoon the pork fat from the frying pan. You save
cooking time, but the dish needs more attention.

Minced Meat

The minced meat (generally beef) which is all ready prepared at supermarkets or in butchers' shops is an excellent buy, for there is no wastage, due to bones and skin. It is generally minced meat from the less expensive cuts, so you must allow sufficient cooking time. Hamburgers and Lamb and Raisin Patties (pages 45 and 41) are meant for prime quality meats, this is why the cooking time is brief.

Remember that minced meat, whether raw or cooked, deteriorates more readily than any other cuts. This is due to the very great expanse of cut surfaces, so always use it quickly even if it has been stored in the refrigerator. Minced meat, as other meats, freezes well whether it is cooked or uncooked. To prepare minced beef for a quick and easy stew with a very mild flavour, follow the directions at the beginning of Moussaka on page 42, but increase the amount of liquid slightly. For a mixture that is full of interest and flavour see the recipes on the next page.

Minced meat makes an excellent meat loaf, and while this takes a little time to cook, it needs the minimum of attention and preparation.

Tomato Meat Loaf

Cut a slice of bread weighing about 2 oz., put this into a basin and add $\frac{1}{4}$ pint ($\frac{2}{3}$ cup) tomato juice. Stand for a while then mash with a fork (this is much quicker than making breadcrumbs). Add $1\frac{1}{2}$ lb. raw minced meat and a chopped, grated or minced onion. Mix thoroughly, then stir in a good pinch dried herbs, seasoning and 1 egg. Grease a 2 lb. oblong tin and put in the mixture. Cover the top with greased foil, stand in a tin of water (to prevent drying) and cook for $1\frac{1}{4}$ hours in the centre of a very moderate oven, 325°F, Gas Mark 3. Serve hot or cold.
Serves 5–6.

Beef Risotto Milanaise

2 tablespoons oil
2 onions
1–2 cloves garlic
1 lb. minced beef
1 medium-sized can tomatoes
4 carrots

seasoning
1 bay leaf
8 oz. (1 cup) long grain rice
1 pint (2⅔ cups) water
1 tablespoon tomato purée
Garnish:
parsley

Heat the oil in a pan. Peel and cut the onions into thin rings and slice the garlic. Toss the onions and garlic in the oil until the onions are transparent. Put a few rings on one side for garnish. Add the beef to the pan, stir well to break up any lumps. Add the tomatoes and the liquid from the can, the roughly chopped carrots, the tomato purée, seasoning and bay leaf. Cook gently in a covered pan for 45 minutes, stirring once or twice.

Put the rice and the cold water into a saucepan with $\frac{1}{2}$–1 teaspoon salt. Bring the water to the boil, stir briskly then cover the pan. Lower the heat and cook for approximately 15 minutes until the rice is tender and the liquid absorbed. Fork the rice on to a hot dish. Spoon the beef mixture in the centre and garnish with onion rings and a sprig of parsley.
Serves 4–5.

Variations:
Omit a little of the juice from the canned tomatoes and use red wine instead or if you like to use all the liquid from the can plus red wine, blend 1 tablespoon flour into the onion, garlic and meat mixture before blending in the tomatoes, etc.
Country Hotpot: Prepare the meat mixture as the basic recipe, but only cook for 25 minutes, then put into a deep casserole. Cover with thinly sliced raw potatoes and a little seasoning and margarine. Bake for 45 minutes to 1 hour in the centre of a very moderate to moderate oven, 325–350°F, Gas Mark 3–4. Top with chopped parsley.
Serves 4–5.

Using Cooked Meats

As you walk round the supermarket or shops today there is an almost bewildering variety of cooked meats – ham, tongue, sausages of various kinds, salami etc. Most of these are excellent served cold with salads, but many of the cooked meats can be served hot.

Here are some quick suggestions for using the less usual cooked meats, you will find ideas for tongue dishes on page 54.

Salami Fritters

12 oz. salami (choose a fairly tender type such as Mortadella)
1 egg
2 oz. ($\frac{1}{2}$ cup) flour
seasoning
barely $\frac{1}{4}$ pint ($\frac{2}{3}$ cup) tomato juice
oil or fat for frying

Remove the skin from the sliced salami. Blend the egg yolk, flour, seasoning and tomato juice to make a smooth batter. Whisk the egg white and fold in just before coating the salami. Dip the slices in the tomato batter and fry until crisp on both sides in the hot oil or fat. Serve with salad.
Serves 4–5.

Oriental Casserole

2 onions
2 cooking apples
2–3 tomatoes
4–8 oz. mushrooms
6 oz. can Danish 'bacon grill'
2 oz. ($\frac{1}{4}$ cup) fat
$\frac{1}{4}$ pint ($\frac{2}{3}$ cup) water
3 teaspoons Mango chutney
seasoning

Peel and slice or dice the onions and apples, halve the tomatoes. Wash and slice the mushrooms and dice the 'bacon grill'. Heat the fat in the pan and fry the meat, onions, apples and mushrooms for 5 minutes. Add the water, chutney and seasoning and simmer for 3–4 minutes, then put in the tomatoes and heat through.
Serve with green salad and boiled rice.
Serves 4–6.

ORIENTAL CASSEROLE *(Photograph: Plumrose Ltd.)*

Using Cooked Tongue

While ox-tongue is the kind you will generally see for slicing, remember you can buy cans of lambs' and calves' tongues and these have an excellent flavour; they are more mild than ox-tongue and lend themselves admirably to various ways of heating.

If you wish to serve the tongue hot be careful you do not add too much salt to the heating liquid (avoid using very highly seasoned stock cubes for example) for the tongues are generally ready-salted. The recipes below use 12 oz.–1 lb. cooked tongue.

Tongue Florentine:
Slice the tongue or tongues fairly thickly. Put into a saucepan with a little milk, heat gently. Meanwhile cook $1-1\frac{1}{2}$ lb. fresh or frozen spinach, drain carefully. Chop the spinach and mix with a knob of butter and seasoning; arrange round the edge of an oven-proof dish. Lift out the hot tongue and arrange in the centre of the dish. Measure the cooking liquid and make up to $\frac{1}{2}$ pint ($1\frac{1}{3}$ cups). Blend this with $\frac{1}{2}$ oz. cornflour, put into a saucepan with 1 tablespoon butter or margarine and heat gently, stirring well. Add seasoning and a pinch grated or ground nutmeg. Pour over the tongue, top with chopped parsley.
Serves 4–5.

You can make the same dish with canned or cooked asparagus instead of spinach, in which case add a beaten egg to the sauce when it has thickened and simmer gently.

Tongue in cherry sauce:
Slice the tongue or tongues. Open a medium can of red cherries; drain off the cooking liquid. Add a little stock to make this up to $\frac{1}{2}$ pint ($1\frac{1}{3}$ cups), or use water with a $\frac{1}{4}$ of a stock cube; all cherry juice is inclined to be insipid. Blend the liquid with 1 tablespoon cornflour and pour into a frying pan or large shallow pan. Add 1 oz. margarine and simmer gently, stirring well. Add 2 tablespoons red or port wine, the slices of tongue and the cherries, and heat.
Serves 4–5.

Tongue Niçoise:
Blend $\frac{1}{2}$ pint ($1\frac{1}{3}$ cups) tomato juice with 1 tablespoon cornflour. Pour into a frying pan or large shallow pan. Flavour with garlic salt and a little sherry. Add the sliced tongue and heat.

Quick Flavourings with Canned Steak

Mix the steak with a little paprika, heat with sliced cooked potatoes and tomatoes for a quick goulash.
Blend the steak with curry powder to taste. Heat gently, add a few raisins, desiccated coconut, chutney and lemon juice for a curry.
Fry a sliced onion (and sliced mushrooms, if liked) in a little butter, add the canned steak, heat, stir in about $\frac{1}{4}$ pint ($\frac{2}{3}$ cup) dairy soured cream or thin cream and lemon juice. This makes a good quick Beef Stroganoff.
Serve with noodles.

Using Cooked Ham

Cooked ham or boiled bacon is an excellent addition to many dishes. The recipes on the previous pages are just as suitable for ham as they are for tongue.

The traditional accompaniment to ham is the Cumberland sauce below but if you wish to heat slices of ham increase the stock (or water flavoured with a small portion of stock cube) to $\frac{1}{2}$ pint ($1\frac{1}{3}$ cups). This allows for the evaporation as the slices of ham are warmed through.

Cumberland Sauce

2 small oranges
1 lemon
$\frac{1}{4}$ pint ($\frac{2}{3}$ cup) water
2 teaspoons arrowroot or cornflour
$\frac{1}{4}$ pint ($\frac{2}{3}$ cup) ham or white stock

2 teaspoons made mustard
2 tablespoons port wine
4–5 tablespoons redcurrant jelly
seasoning

This sauce is an ideal accompaniment to hot or cold ham or boiled bacon. There are many ways of making it but the sauce should contain orange and lemon juice, redcurrant jelly, mustard and port wine. I find this recipe particularly good.

Cut the peel from the oranges. Remove the white pith then cut into thin matchsticks. A very little lemon rind may be treated in the same way if wished. Squeeze the juice from the fruits. Put the rind into a pan with the cold water. Soak for 1 hour then simmer very gently in a covered pan until nearly tender (about 15–20 minutes). Remove the lid towards the end of the cooking time so the liquid is reduced to 3 tablespoons. Blend the arrowroot or cornflour with the ham or white stock. Put into the pan with the fruit juice, mustard, wine and jelly. Stir over a low heat until thickened and clear. Season well. Serve hot or cold.
Serves 4–5.

Cooking Chicke

*The modern frying chickens are ideal for quick cooking, indeed they are
so young and tender that over-cooking spoils both texture and flavour.
If you buy frozen chicken portions it is better to allow these to thaw out at
room temperature, to dry them well, then to use as ordinary chicken portions.*

To fry young chickens:
Divide a small chicken into 4 portions, 2 breast and wing
joints and 2 leg joints (or if very small split as the Spatchcock
of Chicken on page 59. Dry the joints well, then coat in
seasoned flour or beaten egg, diluted with a little water and
breadcrumbs. In view of the cooking time, soft fine
breadcrumbs are better than the crisped variety. Cook
quickly on either side in hot butter (mixed with a little oil to
prevent the butter becoming dark) or hot fat or oil. When the
chicken is brown lower the heat and cook gently until tender.
The total cooking time is about 15 minutes. Drain and serve
with salad or vegetables.

Fried Chicken and Oranges

4 portions young chicken	2 oz. ($\frac{1}{4}$ cup) butter
1 oz. ($\frac{1}{4}$ cup) flour	$\frac{1}{2}$ tablespoon oil
seasoning	3 large oranges

Dry the portions of chicken and coat in seasoned flour. Heat
the butter and oil in a pan. Fry the chicken as above until
nearly tender. Squeeze the juice from 2 oranges, pour over
the chicken and finish cooking. Serve the chicken joints on a
bed of boiled rice and garnish with the remaining orange,
peeled and cut into rings.
Serves 4.

Variation:
This is even more delicious if 2–3 tablespoons halved
walnuts are added to the pan with the orange juice. The
combination of crisp nuts and orange juice is very pleasant.

To Grill Chicken

Young chickens are equally as good grilled as fried. Either divide the chicken, as in the traditional dish – Spatchcock of Chicken, see page 59 – or cut it into 4 joints.
Chicken dries easily and must be kept well moistened during cooking, so melt 2–3 oz. butter or use oil and brush the chicken before and during cooking. Allow a total cooking time of about 15 minutes. Pre-heat the grill. Put the chicken under the heat, brown quickly on one side, turn and brown on the second side, then lower the heat and continue cooking until tender.
Chicken may be given additional flavour by adding any of the following to the butter or oil:
grated lemon rind and juice; curry powder and Worcestershire sauce to taste; crushed garlic and chopped lemon thyme and parsley; 1 tablespoon made mustard and a few drops Tabasco sauce.

Spatchcock of Chicken

4 very small young chickens or
  2 larger ones
seasoning
2 oz. ($\frac{1}{4}$ cup) butter

grated rind 1 lemon
Garnish:
watercress
lemon

Split the chickens right down the backbone, so they open out quite flat. Mix the seasoning with the melted butter, add the lemon rind. Grill the chickens until tender, basting with the butter as they cook. Garnish with watercress and sliced lemon.
Serves 4.

Variation:
Very young pigeons or partridges may be cooked in the same way. Omit the lemon if wished and flavour the butter with a few drops Worcestershire sauce and a pinch curry powder.

Using Frozen Chicken Breasts

The breasts of frozen chicken lend themselves to delicious and delicately flavoured dishes. Always allow these to defrost, if possible, so they may be patted dry before using.

Chicken Cordon Bleu

4 chicken breasts
4 slices ham
4 slices Gruyère cheese
$\frac{1}{2}$ oz. flour

Coating:
1 egg
2 oz. soft breadcrumbs
oil or fat for frying

Dry the chicken breasts well, then slit these to make a 'pocket'. Insert the slices of ham and cheese into this. Mix a little seasoning with the flour and dust the chicken breasts with this. Coat in beaten egg and crumbs and fry steadily in the oil or fat until crisp, golden brown and tender. This takes about 12–15 minutes. Serve at once with salad.
Serves 4.

Variations:
Chicken Rossini: Fill the chicken breasts with pâté and finely diced uncooked mushrooms instead of ham and cheese. Coat and fry as above.
Russian chicken: Blend a little made mustard with 2 oz. ($\frac{1}{4}$ cup) butter. Add 1 tablespoon finely chopped onion, 1 tablespoon finely diced green pepper and 2 tablespoons neatly sliced mushrooms. Press this mixture into the chicken breasts, then coat and fry as above.
Chicken in soured cream sauce: Do not coat or fill the chicken breasts. Simply fry until golden brown in a little butter. Lift out of the pan, add finely diced onion and mushrooms and fry for 2–3 minutes. Pour in $\frac{1}{2}$ pint ($1\frac{1}{3}$ cups) dairy soured cream and season well. Replace the chicken breasts and heat until tender.

60

To Stew Chicken

If using young chicken for stewing, do take care not to over-cook and to make a fairly rich sauce (i.e. be generous with the fat — whatever kind you use — so the chicken is kept moist).

The following suggestions provide 2 completely different chicken dishes, both cooked in a short time. It is assumed you will be using a jointed chicken; if you prefer to use a whole young chicken then the time will be considerably more. All quantities are for 4 portions of chicken, so divide a chicken as instructed on page 58.

Fricassee of chicken:

Put the chicken joints into a pan with just enough water to cover, 1–2 chopped onions (or the equivalent in dehydrated onion), seasoning and a pinch dried or fresh herbs and simmer very gently for 25 minutes.

Meanwhile heat $1\frac{1}{2}$ oz. butter in a pan, stir in $1\frac{1}{2}$ oz. flour, cook gently for 2–3 minutes, then gradually blend in $\frac{1}{2}$ pint ($1\frac{1}{3}$ cups) milk and the same amount of liquid from the pan (do this with a large spoon, so there is no possibility of scalding yourself). Bring the sauce to the boil and cook until smooth and thickened. Add seasoning, 1–2 tablespoons dry sherry or lemon juice. Lift the chicken out of the pan and coat with the sauce. Garnish with sliced fried mushrooms and cooked rice or creamed potatoes and mixed diced vegetables. **Serves 4.**

Chicken Chasseur:

Chop 1–2 onions and 1–2 cloves garlic (optional) and fry in 2 oz. ($\frac{1}{4}$ cup) margarine or fat. Add a medium sized can of tomatoes, seasoning and a little chopped parsley and/or chopped herbs. Simmer for a few minutes. Add $\frac{1}{4}$ pint ($\frac{2}{3}$ cup) chicken stock or water and $\frac{1}{2}$ chicken stock cube. Place the pieces of chicken in the sauce, cover the pan and simmer for 25 minutes. Serve with a green vegetable. If you increase the amount of margarine or fat to 3 oz. ($\frac{3}{8}$ cup) and fry the chicken portions until brown, remove and then fry the onions etc., you will have a pleasant appearance and flavour to this dish. **Note:** Garlic salt makes a speedy substitute for garlic.

Using Ready Cooked Chicken

The barbecued or ready cooked chickens one can buy are ideal for a quick meal, but probably after a time you will feel you would like a change of flavour. The following recipes enable you to produce unusual dishes with cooked chicken in a matter of minutes. Cooked turkey could be used as an alternative in some recipes; if buying this ready sliced it would be advisable to request thick slices, so the delicate flesh does not dry too much in heating.

Coq au Vin

2–4 oz. small mushrooms
1 oz. butter or margarine
1 tablespoon flour
$\frac{1}{2}$ pint ($1\frac{1}{3}$ cups) white wine or use half wine and half chicken stock*

2–3 tablespoons cocktail onions
seasoning
1 cooked chicken
Garnish:
chopped parsley

*or water and $\frac{1}{4}-\frac{1}{2}$ chicken stock cube.

Toss the mushrooms in the hot butter or margarine. Blend the flour with the wine, add to the mushrooms and stir gently until thickened. Put in the well drained onions, a little seasoning and simmer for a few minutes. Meanwhile, heat the whole chicken for a short time in the oven (do not over-heat). Put on to a dish and pour the sauce over this and top with parsley.
Serves 4.

Variations:
Joint the chicken or cut slices of turkey into fingers and heat in the hot sauce; in this case use a little extra liquid, as some will evaporate as the chicken heats. Use half wine and half milk to make a creamier type sauce. Use all red wine or half red wine and half stock, do not blend milk with the red wine, but stir 1–2 tablespoons thick cream into the thickened sauce. Use dehydrated or sliced onions in place of the cocktail onions.

Sausage and Chicken Cutlets

1 lb. sausagemeat
1 tablespoon chopped parsley
2 tablespoons finely chopped raw
  mushrooms
1 cooked chicken
Garnish:
watercress

halved tomatoes
1 tablespoon water
2–3 oz. crisp breadcrumbs
2 oz. ($\frac{1}{4}$ cup) fat or oil for frying
Coating:
1 egg

Blend the sausagemeat with the chopped parsley and the
mushrooms. Divide into 8 pieces. Cut the chicken into
8 portions, i.e. 2 from each leg and 2 from each breast and
wing. Take out as many bones as you can, without wasting
any of the flesh. Mould the sausagemeat mixture round the
chicken to form a neat round or cutlet shape. Mix the egg
and water, brush over the sausagemeat coating and then roll
in the breadcrumbs. Heat the fat or oil in a frying pan and fry
the cutlets until crisp and golden brown. Drain on absorbent
paper and arrange on a dish with the watercress and halved
tomatoes. Serve hot or cold.
Serves 4 as a main dish or 8 as a light snack.

Variations:
Cut turkey into fairly solid 'wedges', coat in seasoned flour,
then the sausagemeat, egg and crumbs. The sausagemeat
would not cling so easily to the flesh of turkey without the
flour coating.
To make a more interesting dish make a small 'pocket' in the
pieces of chicken and insert a little pâté or cranberry jelly.
Uncooked chicken portions can be used in exactly the same
way, but this means rapidly browning to crisp the outside
sausagemeat, then lowering the heat so that the raw chicken
is cooked adequately.

To Roast Chicken

The recipe that follows gives the timing for young chickens. It is better to choose 2 smaller birds, to save cooking time, rather than one large bird. Omit sauce in recipe below and serve with sausages and bacon.

Roasted Poussins

4 small spring chickens
small can sweet corn
1 tablespoon chopped chives or
  spring onions
3 oz. ($\frac{3}{8}$ cup) butter
seasoning
Sauce:
1 tablespoon chicken fat
1 level tablespoon cornflour

pinch paprika
$\frac{1}{2}$ pint + 2 tablespoons thin cream
  or cream and chicken stock
1 egg yolk
1 tablespoon sherry
Garnish:
red pepper (pimento)

Stuff the chickens with well-drained sweet corn blended with the chopped chives or spring onions and a $\frac{1}{3}$ of the butter. Melt rest of butter and pour over the chickens, roast until tender, this takes about 45 minutes in a moderately hot to hot oven, 400°F, Gas Mark 5–6. Lift the small chickens on to a hot serving dish and keep hot.
Spoon 1 tablespoon of the fat from the roasting tin into a saucepan.
Blend the cornflour and paprika with the fat, cook for 2–3 minutes, stirring all the time. Gradually stir $\frac{1}{2}$ pint ($1\frac{1}{3}$ cups) thin cream, or cream and stock, into the 'roux'. Bring slowly to the boil, stirring until thickened. Remove from the heat and add the egg yolk, blended with 2 tablespoons cream and sherry. Return to a very low heat and cook, without boiling, for a few minutes. Season well. Spoon the sauce over the spring chickens, garnish with red pepper (pimento) and serve.
Serves 4 or 8 depending upon the size of the spring chickens. The poussins can be served on a bed of Speedy Ratatouille (page 74) which makes a delicious and unusual accompaniment.

Following page: WHITE SAUCE

Sauces

A sauce adds interest and extra food value to many dishes. One of the basic sauces is given on page 69, with suggestions for quicker methods of preparing this.
When you need a savoury sauce very quickly, heat mayonnaise in a basin over hot water, then add a little top of the milk or thin cream to make the sauce less 'biting'.
Make use of the many excellent canned or dehydrated sauces on the market.

Aurora sauce:
Mix a little cream, paprika pepper, a pinch of dried tarragon, a shake of garlic or onion salt and a few drops of anchovy essence and add to warmed mayonnaise, home-made or ready-prepared white sauce.
This is delicious with white fish.

Bonne Femme sauce:
Add sliced fried or canned mushrooms to homemade or ready-prepared white sauce, together with an egg yolk blended with a little cream and a few drops of white wine vinegar. Heat gently. This is excellent with boiled chicken.

Bulgarian sauce:
Blend well drained and chopped canned tomatoes with diced celery, seasoning and garlic salt or crushed garlic. Serve with cold ham or tongue.

Washington sauce:
Mix equal quantities of apple sauce and fresh or canned tomato purée, season well and add a few drops of lemon juice. Serve with cold pork or ham.

Tartare sauce:
Add chopped parsley, capers and gherkins to mayonnaise or salad dressing.

Yoghourt sauces:
Natural yoghourt can be flavoured with lemon juice, chopped herbs, curry powder, etc. to serve as a dressing over salads or it can be warmed gently as a sauce over chicken, etc. Soured cream can be used in the same way.

Preceding page: BONNE FEMME SAUCE *(Photograph: Colman's Sauce Mixes)*

White Sauce

Coating consistency:
1 oz. butter or margarine
1 oz. (1¼ cup) flour

½ pint milk
seasoning

Heat the butter and margarine, do not over-heat. Remove from the heat, stir in the flour. Return to a low heat and stir for several minutes, until the 'roux' forms a dry looking ball. Once again take the pan off the heat and gradually blend in the liquid. Stir briskly with a wooden spoon as you do so. Return once again to the heat and bring steadily to the boil, stirring or whisking all the time as the sauce thickens. Add a little seasoning and continue stirring for 4–5 minutes, until the sauce coats the back of the spoon, see the picture on page 66. Taste and add more seasoning if required.
Serves 3–4.

There are three ways in which the sauce may be made more rapidly:
Blending method: Use the same proportions as above. Blend the flour carefully with the liquid. Put into a saucepan. Add the butter or margarine. Bring gradually to the boil, stirring all the time. Continue cooking as above.
Quick method: Use the same proportions as above. Prepare the 'roux'. Take the pan off the heat, add all the liquid. Return to the heat. Allow the liquid to come to the boil and whisk sharply. Continue cooking as above.
Using cornflour: You can use cornflour instead of flour but remember it thickens more than flour, so use ½ oz. in place of 1 oz. (¼ cup) flour. Although a sauce made with cornflour thickens more quickly than one made with flour, it is important to cook it for some minutes.

Variations:
Add a little anchovy essence; chopped parsley or other herbs; 2–4 oz. (⅓–⅔ cup) chopped shrimps; 4 oz. (1 cup) grated Cheddar cheese (added when the sauce has thickened).

Rice and Pasta
Using Pasta

All pasta cooks within a relatively short time, but there are specially produced 'quick cooking' varieties which save a few minutes. Do not over-cook these, or any pasta, otherwise you lose so much of the texture (the pasta becomes limp and watery) and the flavour.

Many of the prepared canned or dehydrated sauces can be heated or prepared while the pasta is cooking, for example try: macaroni with curry sauce; spaghetti with a cheese or tomato or meat (Bolognese) sauce.

Spaghetti à la Napolitaine

6–8 oz. spaghetti
seasoning
Parmesan cheese
little butter
medium can tomatoes

1 tablespoon tomato purée
8 oz. cooked ham
little chopped parsley

Cook the spaghetti in boiling salted water (allow at least 3 pints water to the smaller quantity of pasta) until tender, strain then toss with grated Parmesan cheese and butter. Meanwhile heat the canned tomatoes with the purée, add the diced ham, parsley and seasoning. Spoon the spaghetti on to a hot dish and top with the tomato sauce.
Serves 4–5.

Spaghetti à la Reine

Cook the spaghetti as above, strain, tip back into the pan, add a little butter, diced cooked chicken, enough beef stock to moisten and grated cheese. Heat for a few minutes then serve with more grated cheese.

Macaroni Cardinal

6–8 oz. macaroni
seasoning
Sauce:
2 oz. ($\frac{1}{4}$ cup) margarine or butter
1 small onion
$\frac{3}{4}$ pint (2 cups) milk
1 oz. ($\frac{1}{4}$ cup) flour
1 teaspoon paprika
few drops anchovy essence

small crab or lobster* or can of
  crabmeat or lobster
few shelled prawns
few prepared mussels
Garnish:
little melted butter
chopped parsley
paprika
1 lemon

*Choose a female lobster with the red coral (roe)

Put the macaroni into boiling salted water (allow at least
3 pints water to the smaller quantity of pasta); cook until just
tender, then strain.
Meanwhile heat the margarine or butter in another saucepan,
add the finely chopped or grated onion, turn in the margarine
or butter for 2–3 minutes. Add most of the milk, cover the
pan and simmer gently for about 8 minutes. Blend the flour
with the paprika into the remaining milk and stir in the onion
and milk mixture, continue stirring until thickened, add the
anchovy essence, seasoning, flaked crabmeat or lobster (plus
the roe) together with the prawns and mussels, heat for
2–3 minutes only.
Spoon into the centre of a dish. Toss the macaroni in melted
butter, arrange round the sauce, top with chopped parsley,
a sprinkling of paprika and small pieces of lemon.
Serves 4–5.

Variations:
Use flaked white fish instead of crab or lobster; add the
prawns and mussels or omit these.
Diced ham and canned sweet corn can be substituted for fish;
add to the sauce as above.
Top the dish with grated Parmesan cheese.
Note: It is a good idea to prepare an extra quantity of lightly
cooked pasta. Keep it well covered then freshen by putting it
into cold water. Bring to the boil quickly then strain.

Using Rice

Rice is an ideal food when you are short of time. It needs no pre-preparation – most modern rice is ready-washed. It also is possible to buy 'boil in the bag' rice, which is even more labour saving. Cooked rice can be served as an accompaniment to many meat or fish dishes.

Rice Espagnole

2 cloves garlic
2 onions
4 oz. mushrooms
2–3 tomatoes
2 oz. ($\frac{1}{4}$ cup) margarine or use oil
  if wished
8 oz. (1 cup) long grain rice

$\frac{1}{4}$ pint ($\frac{2}{3}$ cup) dry sherry
$\frac{3}{4}$ pint (2 cups) chicken stock or
  water and chicken stock cube
about 12 oz. cooked chicken
seasoning
Garnish:
olives

Crush the garlic, peel and slice the onions and halve the mushrooms (wash these but do not peel them). Cut the tomatoes into fairly large pieces. Toss the vegetables in the hot margarine or oil for a few minutes. Add the rice, mix with the vegetables, then pour in the sherry and stock or water and stock cube. Bring slowly to the boil, stirring well until the mixture comes to the boil. Lower the heat and simmer gently for 15 minutes.
Add the diced chicken and plenty of seasoning and heat for a further 10 minutes. Top with olives and serve at once.
Serves 4–5.

Variations:
Lamb Espagnole: Use the recipe above, adding diced cooked lamb instead of chicken. Add 2–3 tablespoons pine or other nuts just before serving.
Use uncooked chicken or lamb and cook this with the vegetables (use more margarine or oil).

Curried Rice and Prawns

1 large onion
1 small dessert apple
2 oz. ($\frac{1}{4}$ cup) margarine or butter
1 tablespoon curry powder
8 oz. (1 cup) long grain rice
1 tablespoon tomato purée or
  ketchup
$\frac{3}{4}$ pint (2 cups) water or chicken
  stock*
seasoning
1 carrot (optional)

about 8 oz. shelled prawns
Accompaniments:
1 green pepper
2 tomatoes
1 lemon
desiccated coconut
chutney
raisins
olives and/or gherkins
blanched almonds or other nuts

*Chicken stock blends well with shell fish

Peel and slice the onion (or use dehydrated onion). Peel and
chop the apple. Heat the onion and apple in the hot margarine
or butter, then stir in the curry powder and the rice, cook for
2–3 minutes, stirring well. Add the tomato purée or ketchup
and the water or stock. Bring to the boil and cook steadily for
15 minutes, stirring from time to time. Season well and add
a little sugar or chutney if you like a sweet curry. Stir in the
peeled coarsely grated carrot and prawns and heat for about
5 minutes only.
Pile on to a hot dish and serve with the various
accompaniments. Slice the pepper (discard core and seeds)
and arrange with the sliced tomatoes. Cut the lemon into neat
rings (discard the pips). Serve the other accompaniments
separately.
Serves 4.
Note: It is a good idea to prepare an extra quantity of lightly
cooked rice. Keep it well covered then freshen by putting it
into a small quantity of water or margarine and heat quickly,
strain if necessary.

Vegetable Dishes

One of the golden rules about vegetable cookery, particularly green vegetables, is to cook as rapidly as possible, so you will be achieving an excellent flavour and retaining the maximum of mineral salts and vitamins. Make sure the small amount of water is boiling, shred the vegetables or divide cauliflower into small flowerets. Put into the boiling salted water gradually, so the water never goes off the boil, and boil rapidly until just tender – but never over-cooked – serve as soon as possible. Potatoes are an exception to the rule of rapid cooking – cook these steadily to avoid the outside breaking before the centres are cooked.

When you want to avoid preparing fresh vegetables you can choose between the many canned, dehydrated and frozen varieties, all of which are of excellent quality.

Speedy Ratatouille

medium can tomatoes
2 tablespoons oil
2 onions or equivalent in
   dehydrated onion

1–2 cloves garlic or use garlic salt
1 lb. courgettes
seasoning
parsley

Tip the tomatoes and liquid from the can into a pan. Add the oil and the chopped or dehydrated onions, simmer for a few minutes. Add crushed garlic or garlic salt and unpeeled thinly sliced courgettes. Season well, check there is sufficient liquid in the pan; remember that courgettes are a 'watery' vegetable. Put the lid on the pan, simmer steadily for 30–40 minutes, stirring once or twice. Add a little chopped parsley towards the end of the cooking time. Stir once or twice; add extra parsley when cooked. Serve hot or cold.
Serves 6–8.

Quick Vegetable Dishes

The suggestions that follow are suitable for fresh, canned, frozen or dehydrated vegetables. The term 'cooked' is used throughout but canned vegetables (already pre-cooked) should be heated for a few minutes only.

Asparagus Polonaise:
Top hot asparagus with chopped hard boiled eggs and hot butter.

Aubergine fritters:
Wash the vegetables, peel if wished, slice thinly and coat with seasoned flour or with a very thin batter (see fritter batter, page 102, but add a little extra liquid). Fry in deep or shallow oil, drain on absorbent paper. Delicious served with fish dishes.

Carrots à la paysanne:
Toss cooked carrots in butter, with a little cream, lemon juice and finely chopped chives.

Celery in tomato puree:
Heat canned tomatoes with seasoning and a very little yeast extract. Tip cooked celery into this and heat. Diced cooked celeriac can be used instead, and so can chicory heads.

Cabbage Parmesan:
Toss lightly cooked shredded cabbage in butter and grated Parmesan cheese. Put into a dish, top with a little thick cream, more cheese and a grating of nutmeg.

Cauliflower fritters:
Coat lightly cooked sprigs of cauliflower in the same batter as on page 102 and fry until crisp and golden brown. Broccoli spears may be coated in the same way. This is an excellent way to serve these vegetables with cold meats.

Cucumber:
This is equally as good cooked as it is raw in salads. Slice and simmer in salted water; coat in seasoned flour or butter and fry; cook and mash with butter as a purée. The peel can be left on but this gives a slightly bitter taste.

Courgettes:
These may be fried as cucumber above or split and baked in butter in the oven. Top with scrambled egg and cheese when cooked to make a light supper dish.
Alternatively, simmer in a very well seasoned tomato purée.

Marrow:
This should be peeled, diced (take out the seeds) and cooked as above.

More Vegetable Dishes

Green beans with garlic:
Cook 1 chopped onion plus 2 crushed cloves garlic in a little butter. Add to about 1 lb. cooked green beans (sliced runner, whole French or haricots verts).

Haricot beans mornay:
Toss cooked haricot beans in cheese sauce (page 69) and top with chopped chives and chopped parsley.

Mushrooms à la Provencale:
Open a small can of tomatoes, put into a pan with 1–2 chopped onions (or the equivalent in dehydrated onions). Add 1–2 crushed cloves garlic or a little garlic salt and 8 oz. small button mushrooms. Season well, cover the pan, simmer gently for 10 minutes.

Fried onions:
Peel onions, cut into slices. Separate the slices into rings, dry on absorbent paper. Dip the rings in milk then seasoned flour, fry in deep or shallow oil.

Basque peas:
Blend cooked peas with strips of ham or fried bacon. Heat gently, then top with chopped parsley and chopped mint.

Country style peas:
Toss cooked peas with tiny well drained cocktail onions and butter. Season very well.

Cooking Spinach

Fresh or frozen spinach cooks rapidly and is an extremely successful vegetable as the basis of a meal.
Top cooked spinach with fried or poached eggs; add grated cheese or cheese sauce to make a main meal, or blend with diced ham, cream and butter and serve with cold meats.

Spinach Niçoise

$1\frac{1}{2}$–2 lb. fresh spinach or about
12 oz. packet frozen spinach
salt
3 oz. ($\frac{3}{8}$ cup) butter or margarine
2 tablespoons thick cream

pepper
4 large tomatoes
2 onions
4 oz. (1 cup) grated Cheddar,
    Gruyère or Emmenthal cheese

Cook the spinach with a little salt, or as on the packet of frozen spinach. Strain, either sieve or chop finely. Return to the pan with half the butter or margarine and the cream. Heat gently until a creamy consistency. Add pepper to taste. While the spinach is cooking, prepare the tomato layer. Skin and chop the tomatoes and onions. Heat gently in the remaining butter or margarine until soft. Add the cheese, season with salt and pepper, do not heat again. Put the creamed spinach into a shallow, very hot, heat-proof dish, top with the hot tomato and cheese mixture. Heat for a few minutes under the grill and serve at once.
Serves 4–6.

Variation:
A few seedless raisins may be added to the tomato layer
if wished.
Use cooked sprigged cauliflower or cooked sliced courgettes
instead of spinach.

To save time:
Leave frozen spinach in the saucepan at room temperature for
a while so it thaws out; this saves time and adding extra water.

Quick Potato Dishes

The following recipes can be made with dehydrated potatoes instead of cooked and mashed potatoes or canned potatoes instead of cooked boiled potatoes.

Potato Almond Balls

8 oz. (1 cup) mashed potatoes
3 oz. (¾ cup) blanched finely
   chopped almonds

1 egg
oil or fat for frying

Mix the potatoes with about one third of the nuts. Form into small balls. Coat with beaten egg and the rest of the nuts. Fry in hot oil or fat until crisp and golden brown. Drain on absorbent paper. Serve with chicken or cold meats.
Serves 2–3.

Potatoes au Gratin

about 1 lb. cooked potatoes
little thick cream
seasoning

4 oz. (1 cup) grated Cheddar
   cheese
1 oz. fine breadcrumbs
little butter

Slice the potatoes, put one third into a shallow oven-proof dish, top with a little cream, seasoning and one third of the cheese. Add another two layers of potatoes, cream, seasoning and cheese. Top with breadcrumbs and small knobs of butter, then cook for about 20 minutes in the centre of a moderately hot oven, 400°F, Gas Mark 5–6. Serve with egg dishes.
Serves 4.

Variations:
Add a little chopped ham to each layer.
Add a little chopped crisply fried bacon to each layer.
Potatoes Italienne: Add diced salami and chopped hard boiled egg to each layer. This makes an excellent supper dish.

Quick Salads

If green salad ingredients are prepared, then washed, shaken to extract surplus moisture and put in polythene containers in the refrigerator, it is a matter of minutes to use these as a basis for interesting salads, for they will not need time to drain and crisp.

The term 'cooked' is used very often in the recipes that follow – canned ingredients could be used to save time. The following salads are equally good to serve with cold meat, poultry, fish or other protein foods.

Belgian salad:
Mix chopped heads of chicory with mayonnaise and diced red pepper (discard core and seeds).

Celery salad:
Chop celery and mix with diced dessert apple, mayonnaise, raisins and chopped nuts.

Cucumber and potato salad:
Slice cooked potatoes and cucumber thinly, mix together with mayonnaise to bind, top with chopped parsley and capers.

Spring salad:
Mix cooked broad beans with diced potatoes, chopped spring onions and well seasoned oil and vinegar. Top with natural yoghourt, chopped parsley and a little chopped mint.

Florida salad:
Arrange thin slices of ripe melon on crisp lettuce. Sprinkle with a little sweetened lemon juice.

Sunray salad:
Arrange cooked asparagus tips in a neat design on a bed of shredded lettuce (have the tips towards the edge of the plate). Fill the centre with chopped hard boiled eggs.

Cauliflower salad:
Cook a cauliflower very lightly. Drain and put the sprigs into a basin, flower side uppermost. Leave until cold. Turn out and coat with mayonnaise, flavoured with a little fresh tomato purée, and garnish with chopped hard boiled egg.

Hawaiian salad:
Put well drained pineapple on crisp lettuce, top with finely chopped spring onions.

Russian pyramid:
Mix diced cooked potatoes, carrots, turnips and cooked peas with mayonnaise and parsley. Shape into a pyramid on a bed of lettuce and watercress. Chop hard boiled egg yolks and whites and arrange a ring of yolk, then a ring of white round the colourful pyramid of vegetables.

Ham and Potato Salad

2 oz. ($\frac{1}{4}$ cup) margarine or butter	cooked peas
2 oz. ($\frac{1}{2}$ cup) mushrooms	mayonnaise
about 8–12 oz. new, old	**Garnish:**
or canned potatoes	lettuce
4–8 oz. diced ham	tomatoes

Heat the margarine or butter, fry the sliced mushrooms and allow to cool. Boil the potatoes or drain canned potatoes, dice and mix with the ham, peas, mushrooms and mayonnaise while warm. Allow to cool. Serve on a bed of lettuce with sliced tomatoes.
Serves 4–6.

Variations:
This makes a delicious hot salad if crisply fried bacon or boiled ham is used instead of cold ham; make sure the peas and mushrooms are hot. Toss in the mayonnaise, put on the lettuce, add the raw tomatoes and serve at once. If you want a meatless meal, then increase the amount of peas, to add extra protein, or add diced cheese and/or chopped hard boiled eggs.

Smoked Salmon and Egg Salad

4 eggs
little mayonnaise
about 4 oz. very thinly cut
  smoked salmon
1 lemon
cayenne pepper

seasoning
lettuce
Garnish:
watercress
tomatoes

Hard boil the eggs, remove from the boiling water, plunge into cold water and crack the shells. Remove the shells while the eggs are still warm, as it is easier to mash the yolks. Halve the eggs lengthways. Remove the yolks from the whites carefully, put the yolks into a basin, mix thoroughly with enough mayonnaise to make a soft creamy consistency. Chop the smoked salmon finely and blend with a squeeze lemon juice and a shake cayenne pepper. Put into the whole cases. Season the egg yolk mixture and put into a piping bag with a $\frac{1}{4}$-inch rose (nozzle). Pipe the mixture on top of the smoked salmon and arrange on a bed of lettuce. Garnish with watercress and small wedges of tomato.
Serves 4, or 8 if part of a mixed hors d'oeuvre.

Chicken and Walnut Salad

1 lb. cooked chicken
1 lb. cooked potatoes (preferably
  new)*
4 oz. lean ham

mayonnaise
4–6 oz. walnut halves**
lettuce
parsley

*Cook in their jackets
**Preferably fresh not dried walnuts (remove the skin from the walnuts).

Cut the chicken and potatoes into neat dice (try and use the potatoes when freshly cooked and skin after cooking). Dice the ham. Mix the ingredients with a little mayonnaise and the coarsely chopped walnuts. Pile on to shredded lettuce and top with parsley.
Serves 5–6.

Chicken and Peach Salad

Cooked chicken has a very delicate flavour and a salad has to complement this. The salad shown is an ideal blending of flavours.

1 lettuce
bunch watercress
1–2 heads chicory
about 1 lb. cooked chicken
1 dessert pear
1 lemon

medium can sliced peaches
few fresh or dried dates
mayonnaise (optional)
little oil and vinegar dressing,
    page 12

Arrange the prepared lettuce, watercress and chicory in a bowl. Top with neatly diced pieces of cooked chicken, sliced fresh pear, dipped in oil and vinegar dressing to prevent the pear discolouring. Add well drained sliced canned peaches and fresh or dried dates. Serve with mayonnaise or oil and vinegar dressing and garnish with lemon.
Serves 4–6.

Scrambled egg Salad

Scrambled egg is as delicious when cold as when freshly cooked. Do not over-cook the eggs.

4 eggs
2 tablespoons milk or thin cream
seasoning
$1\frac{1}{2}$ oz. butter

few cooked peas
few anchovy fillets
little mayonnaise
mixed salad

Beat the eggs with the milk or cream and season lightly. Heat the butter and cook the eggs until nearly set, stirring very gently. Take off the heat and add the peas, chopped anchovy fillets and enough mayonnaise to make the mixture the consistency of whipped cream. Pile on the salad.
Serves 3–4.

Swedish Salad

4 rollmop herrings
2 dessert apples
12 oz. cooked or canned potatoes

few gherkins
1 tablespoon capers
mayonnaise

Dice all the ingredients except the gherkins, which should be neatly sliced, and capers, which are left whole. Blend with a little mayonnaise, then flavour with some of the vinegar from the rollmop herrings.
Serves 4–6.

Cheese Salads

All cheeses can be used in salads. For a low calorie salad choose cottage cheese as the main ingredient. For a strong flavour choose one of the veined blue cheeses. Blend sieved or grated cheese with mayonnaise to make an interesting dressing for potato salad or other vegetable salads.

Cauliflower and Cheese Mould

1 small cauliflower
seasoning
3 hard boiled eggs
8 oz. (1 cup) cottage cheese
2 teaspoons capers

4 tablespoons
mayonnaise
few prawns
tomatoes

Cook sprigged cauliflower in seasoned water until just soft. Strain, mix with 2 chopped hard boiled eggs, the cheese, capers and mayonnaise. Spoon neatly on to a dish. Top with the third chopped egg and prawns. Garnish with sliced tomatoes.
Serves 4.

Blue Cheese and Pear Salad

3–4 oz. Blue cheese
little mayonnaise
4 canned pear halves

lettuce
grapes

Blend the crumbled cheese with enough mayonnaise to make a creamy consistency. Arrange the pear halves on a bed of lettuce. Top with the cheese mixture and garnish with de-seeded grapes.
Serves 2.

Variations:
Add chopped nuts to the cheese mixture.
Use grated Cheddar cheese, mixed with seedless raisins, in place of Blue cheese.

More Salads

Many of the salads that follow may be served as a light main dish.

Savoury fruit salad:
Arrange a bed of lettuce and top with segments of orange, grapefruit, dessert apple (dipped in well seasoned oil and vinegar) and de-seeded grapes. Top with natural yogourt, flavoured with chopped herbs. Serve with cream or cottage cheese.

Salad Parmentier:
Mix sliced new potatoes, hard boiled eggs, chopped chives and mayonnaise. Top with chopped parsley and paprika.

German salad:
Mix well drained diced Bismarck herrings, cooked beetroot and cooked potatoes. Serve on a bed of lettuce or endive, garnish with quartered hard boiled egg.

Chasseur salad:
Dice cooked chicken, mix with diced tomatoes, chopped spring onions, sliced raw mushrooms. Mix with mayonnaise and garnish with rings of beetroot and cucumber.

Egg and watercress salad:
Arrange halved hard boiled eggs on watercress. Top with mayonnaise flavoured with horseradish cream. Garnish with red pepper.

Salami salad:
Cut salami into neat strips, grate raw carrots, chop dessert apples. Mix with well seasoned oil and vinegar, put on to lettuce, garnish with black and green olives.

Tongue and asparagus salad:
Cut cooked tongue into neat fingers and mix with chopped celery, diced tomatoes, a very little freshly chopped basil and chopped hard boiled eggs. Put on to a mixed green salad. Top with mayonnaise, garnish with asparagus.

Sausage and bean salad:
Slice cooked sausages, mix with chopped cooked French beans, spring onions and celery. Toss in a little mayonnaise or seasoned oil and vinegar.

Smoked salmon salad:
An excellent way of making a little of this expensive fish go much further. Dice 4 oz. smoked salmon neatly, mix with 8 oz. diced cooked new potatoes, add a little chopped celery, a few chopped well drained anchovy fillets and blend with lemon flavoured mayonnaise. Serve on lettuce and garnish with lemon and hard boiled eggs.

Cheese Dishes

Cheese is such a complete protein food, in fact it is one of the best of the convenience foods for you can eat it without any further preparation. Cheese with bread, biscuits, salad and fruit makes a perfect meal and the selection of cheeses available provides infinite variety.

Cheese Soufflé Slices

4 fairly thick slices of bread
1½ oz. butter or margarine
1½ oz. butter or margarine
5 tablespoons thin cream

1–2 teaspoons made mustard
6 oz. (1½ cups) grated Cheddar
  cheese
3 eggs
seasoning

Spread one side of the bread with butter or margarine and put on to a buttered baking tray. Heat for 5–10 minutes (depending upon the crispness required) towards the top of a hot oven. Meanwhile blend the cream, mustard, cheese, egg yolks and seasoning. Stir briskly until the consistency of a thick cream then fold in the stiffly whisked egg whites. Spoon on to the bread, do not spread to the edges, and set for about 8 minutes in the oven.
Serves 4.

Variations:
Spread the bread and butter with seasoned sliced tomatoes before baking in the oven; heat until tomatoes are tender then top with cheese mixture and bake.
Top the crisped bread with hot fried sliced mushrooms then add the cheese misture and bake.
Heat rounds of creamed potato on oven-proof plates then top with the cheese mixture and bake.

Fried cheese:
Add slices of Dutch, Cheddar or Gruyère cheese to the frying pan or grill when cooking bacon. Heat for 1–2 minutes only.

89

Deep-fried cheese:
Coat segments of Dutch or Camembert cheese in beaten egg and crumbs and deep fry for 1–2 minutes only.

Cheese Fritters

approximately 2 oz. cooked
  macaroni, spaghetti or rice
2 eggs
2 oz. ($\frac{1}{2}$ cup) grated Cheddar
  cheese

seasoning
pinch dried herbs
oil or fat for frying

Cut the macaroni or spaghetti into small pieces. Mix all the ingredients together. Drop spoonfuls into a little hot oil or fat and fry for 1–2 minutes. Turn and fry on the second side. Drain on absorbent paper and serve hot with salad.
Serves 2.

Cheese Kebabs

Dutch cheese, Edam or Gouda, are ideal for these, as they cook well and do not crumble when put on to the metal skewers. Cut the cheese into $\frac{3}{4}$–1 inch cubes. Put on to metal skewers with small mushrooms, tiny firm tomatoes, pieces of green pepper and small cooked onions. Brush with melted butter and cook for a few minutes under a hot grill.

Variations:
Cheese and bacon kebabs: Put diced cheese and small bacon rolls on to the skewers; cook as above.
Cheese and fruit kebabs: Put diced cheese, segments of orange, rings of banana, segments of apple (dipped in lemon juice) on to the skewers; cook as above.

Soufflé Potatoes

1 lb. mashed potatoes
seasoning
2 oz. ($\frac{1}{4}$ cup) butter
4 eggs

6 oz. ($1\frac{1}{2}$ cups) grated Cheddar
cheese
3 tablespoons thick cream

Beat the potatoes with seasoning, butter, 2 egg yolks and 2 oz. ($\frac{1}{2}$ cup) of the cheese. Spread in an oven- proof dish and bake for 15 minutes just above the centre of a moderately hot oven, 400°F, Gas Mark 5–6. Meanwhile beat the remaining yolks with the cream and the cheese until a smooth mixture. Season very well and fold in the stiffly whisked egg whites. Spoon over the potato mixture and bake for a further 15–20 minutes until well risen. Serve with grilled bacon or ham or as a supper dish.
Serves 4.

Tomato and Cheese Pudding

8 oz. can tomatoes
seasoning
2 oz. soft breadcrumbs

2 eggs
4 oz. (1 cup) grated cheese

Heat the tomatoes for a few minutes, breaking them up as much as possible – do not sieve or emulsify; cool slightly. Add the seasoning, breadcrumbs, eggs and grated cheese to the mixture. Beat well then pour into a greased 1–$1\frac{1}{2}$ pint ovenproof dish and bake for 30–35 minutes in the centre of a moderate to moderately hot oven, 375–400°F, Gas Mark 5–6, until well risen and firm. Serve at once.
Serves 4.

Variation:
Use $\frac{1}{2}$ pint ($1\frac{1}{3}$ cups) milk instead of the tomatoes and flavour the mixture with a little Worcestershire sauce before baking.

Pancakes

You can buy excellent pancake mixes, but the traditional recipe is simple to make and can provide the basis for many interesting dishes.

Pancakes

Batter:
4 oz. (1 cup) flour, preferably
  plain
pinch salt

1 egg
$\frac{1}{2}$ pint ($1\frac{1}{3}$ cups) milk or milk and
  water
oil or fat for frying (see method)

Sieve the flour and salt, add the egg and a little milk or milk and water. Beat or whisk thoroughly to give a smooth thick batter. Gradually whisk in the rest of the liquid.

For each pancake you cook, put about 2 teaspoons oil or a knob of fat the size of an unshelled almond into the pan. If using a 'non-stick' pan then brush with oil or melted fat before cooking each pancake. This is essential if you want really crisp pancakes. Heat the oil or fat until a faint blue haze is seen coming from the pan. Pour or spoon in a little batter, then move the pan so the batter flows over the bottom, it should give a paper thin layer. Cook fairly quickly until set on the bottom. This takes about $1\frac{1}{2}$–2 minutes. To test if ready to toss or turn, shake the pan and the pancake should move easily if cooked on the under surface. Toss or turn carefully. Cook for about the same time on the second side. Lift or slide the pancake out of the pan. Keep hot (see below), while cooking the rest of the pancakes. This batter should give enough pancakes for 4 people, but you may be able to serve a greater number if using a substantial filling.

To keep pancakes hot:
Either put a large plate over a pan of boiling water and place each cooked pancake on this or keep hot on an uncovered dish in a cool oven.

Following page: MAKING PANCAKES

Popovers

4 oz. (1 cup) flour*
pinch salt
2 eggs

$\frac{3}{8}$ pint (1 cup) milk
2 teaspoons oil or
melted butter

*Use either self-raising flour or plain flour with 1 level teaspoon baking powder or plain flour with $\frac{1}{4}$ level teaspoon bicarbonate of soda (baking soda) and $\frac{1}{2}$ level teaspoon cream of tartar.

Sieve the flour or flour and raising agent well with the salt. Add the eggs and beat, then gradually whisk in the milk until a smooth batter. Add the oil just before cooking.
Grease really deep patty tins, custard cups or proper Popover tins and heat them for a few minutes in a hot oven, 425–450°F, Gas Mark 6–7. Half fill with the batter and bake in a hot oven for about 20 minutes, then lower the heat to very moderate and cook for a further 15–20 minutes until really crisp and brown. Serve hot immediately.
Makes 8–12.

Saucer Pancakes

2 oz. ($\frac{1}{4}$ cup) butter or margarine
2 oz. ($\frac{1}{4}$ cup) caster sugar
2 eggs
3 oz. ($\frac{3}{4}$ cup) plain flour

$\frac{1}{4}$ pint ($\frac{2}{3}$ cup) milk
2 tablespoons water
fat for greasing

Cream the butter or margarine and sugar. Gradually beat in the eggs, you may find the mixture 'curdles' but that does not matter. Whisk in the flour, milk and water to make a thin batter. Grease and warm large oven-proof saucers or flat dishes in a hot oven. Spoon in the mixture and bake for 15 minutes towards the top of the oven. Serve with hot jam, fruit or lemon and sugar.
Makes 8–12.

Preceding page: POPOVERS *(Photograph: R.H.M. Foods Ltd.)*

Making Pastry

When you are in a hurry take advantage of the very excellent frozen and packet pastries that are available.
As short crust pastry is the easiest and quickest to make, the recipe is given below.
Some of the most interesting 'pastries' can be made with biscuits or with cornflakes or other breakfast cereals, see page 98.

Short Crust Pastry

The standard method of making short crust pastry is:
a) Sieve 8 oz. (2 cups) plain flour with a pinch salt.
b) Rub in 4 oz. ($\frac{1}{2}$ cup) selected fat.
c) Bind with cold water, roll into a ball and use.
Modern developments in the production of vegetable fats, soft (luxury) margarines and oils now make it possible to prepare short crust pastry very quickly. These are the correct methods to use:

With luxury margarine:
a) Weigh out 8 oz. (2 cups) plain flour, sieve with a pinch salt.
b) Put 6 oz. ($\frac{3}{4}$ cup) luxury margarine with 2 tablespoons of the sieved flour and 2 tablespoons water into a bowl then cream well with a wooden spoon.
c) Stir in the remainder of the sieved flour and salt and blend. Roll into a ball and use.
Note: If you prefer to use only 4 oz. ($\frac{1}{2}$ cup) of the margarine then increase the water to about 3 tablespoons.

With white vegetable fat:
a) Sieve 8 oz. (2 cup) plain flour and a pinch salt into a bowl.
b) Add 4 oz. ($\frac{1}{2}$ cup) fat and 2 tablespoons water.
c) Blend with a fork. Roll into a ball and use.
Note: You will need a generous amount of flour on the pastry board to counteract the rather rich texture of the pastry.

With oil:
a) Put 5 tablespoons oil and $2\frac{1}{2}$ tablespoons water into a bowl.
b) Whisk until the mixture turns opaque.
c) Gradually add the sieved 8 oz. (2 cups) plain flour and pinch salt, mixing with a metal spoon. Roll into a ball and use.
Note: If the pastry (made by any method) seems a little dry, do not add extra water, simply handle with damp hands.

Uncooked Pastries

These 'pastries' can be allowed to set in a cool place. If you heat the mixture the 'pastry' becomes more crisp.

Fillings for these pastries:
The pastry below makes an excellent flan case. Fill with ice cream, or drained canned or cooked or raw fruit. To glaze fruit, warm 4 tablespoons redcurrant jelly with a little fruit juice or water, cool slightly, brush over the fruit.
Fill a savoury flan with cheese sauce plus cooked vegetables; cream or cottage cheese blended with diced ham or shell fish.

Cornflake Flan

2 oz. ($\frac{1}{4}$ cup) butter or margarine
2 oz. ($\frac{1}{4}$ cup) caster sugar
2 teaspoons golden syrup
4 oz. (good 3 cups) slightly crushed Cornflakes

Filling:
fruit or ice cream
Decoration:
cream (optional)

Cream the butter or margarine, sugar and syrup. Add the Cornflakes. Form into a flan shape. Either set in a cool place for a short time or brown for 10 minutes in a very moderate oven. Fill as suggestions above and decorate with cream.
Serves 4.

BISCUIT CRUMB FLAN *(Photograph: Chiltonian Ltd.)*

Variations:
Use other breakfast cereals in place of Cornflakes. Omit the golden syrup. This gives a firmer textured crust.
Biscuit crumb pastry: Use crushed plain, semi-sweet or sweet biscuit crumbs instead of Cornflakes.

If you want a savoury flan omit both sugar and syrup, use plain biscuit crumbs or Cornflakes and season well.
For extra flavour use ginger-nut crumbs (excellent with apple or pear fillings) or chocolate wholemeal biscuit crumbs. This makes a very delicious crust for an ice cream filling.

Using Ready-Prepared Pastry

The frozen pastry and packets of pre-prepared pastry are of very high quality and can save a great deal of preparation time. Follow the packet directions for defrosting, or mixing, and remember that when a recipe planned for home-made pastry states 8 oz. pastry, it does not mean the total weight of pastry but pastry made with that amount of flour, so:
8 oz. short crust pastry *means* 12 oz. ready-prepared pastry (8oz. (2 cups) flour plus 4 oz. ($\frac{1}{2}$ cup) fat, etc.)
8 oz. puff pastry *means* 1 lb. ready-prepared pastry (8 oz. (2 cups) flour plus 8 oz. (1 cup butter, etc.)

Apple Cream Slices:
Use 9 oz. ready-prepared short crust pastry, or pastry made with 6 oz. (1$\frac{1}{2}$ cups) flour, etc. Roll out thinly to form a neat oblong; prick well and bake for about 20 minutes in the centre of a hot oven until golden brown. Allow to cool.
Make up 1 pint (2$\frac{2}{3}$ cups) lemon flavoured jelly with only $\frac{1}{2}$ pint (1$\frac{1}{3}$ cups) very hot water. When this is cold and beginning to stiffen slightly fold in 12 tablespoons thick smooth sweetened apple purée and $\frac{1}{4}$ pint ($\frac{2}{3}$ cup) whipped cream. Spread the pastry with apricot jam then with the half stiffened jelly mixture. When quite firm cut into fingers with a sharp knife dipped in hot water. Decorate as liked.
Makes about 12.

Easy Desserts

Some of the easiest and quickest desserts are those based upon fruit.
If you like fritters you will find the basic recipe overleaf. Instead of apples
try bananas, canned or fresh pineapple rings or large plums.
When cooking fruit or making a fruit purée save some for quick desserts or
sauces to serve with ice cream, etc.

Caramelled Rice

large can creamed rice*
$\frac{1}{4}$ pint ($\frac{2}{3}$ cup) thick or thick and
  thin cream

3 tablespoons brown sugar
2 tablespoons blanched flaked
  almonds

* Use cold creamy cooked rice.

Blend the rice and whipped cream. Put into a shallow
flame-proof serving dish. Top with the sugar and nuts and
heat gently under the grill until golden brown. Serve cold.
Serves 4–5.

Variation:
Add diced well drained canned, cooked or fresh apricots,
pineapple or oranges to the rice.

Diplomat Pudding

1 pint ($2\frac{2}{3}$ cups) thick sweet
  custard
3 macaroon biscuits
2 bananas

red currant jelly
$\frac{1}{4}$ pint ($\frac{2}{3}$ cup) thick or mixed cream

Mix the custard with sliced macaroons and bananas. Spoon
into the serving dish. Top with a layer of red currant jelly
and lightly whipped cream.
Serves 4–6.

Fritter Batter

4 oz. (1 cup) flour (preferably plain)
pinch salt
2 eggs

$\frac{1}{4}$ pint ($\frac{2}{3}$ cup) milk or milk and water
1–2 teaspoons melted butter or oil

Sieve the flour and salt. Gradually beat in the eggs and liquid to form a smooth batter. Add butter or oil just before cooking. For a lighter texture separate the eggs. Add the yolks to the flour, then the milk and butter or oil. Fold the stiffly beaten egg whites into the mixture just before coating the fruit. Economical batter: Use one egg only.

Apple Fritters

fritter batter (above)
1 tablespoon flour
pan deep fat or oil for frying or 3–4 oz. fat for shallow frying

4 good-sized cooking apples
sugar to coat

Prepare the batter as the recipe in a large basin (this makes it easier to coat the fruit). Put the flour on a large plate. Heat deep fat or oil – test if correct temperature: a cube of bread should turn golden in 30 seconds. Lower the heat so the fat or oil does not over-heat. Peel and core apples, cut into $\frac{1}{2}$-inch rings.
Coat the fruit first with flour (this makes sure the batter adheres well) and then with the batter. Lift out with a fork, hold over the basin and allow surplus to drop into the basin. Drop into the hot fat or oil, cook steadily for 4–5 minutes until golden brown. Lift out, drain on absorbent paper, coat in sugar and serve hot.
If frying in shallow fat, heat this as you coat the fruit. Turn the fritters after 2–3 minutes and brown other side.
Serves 4.

Tipsy Fingers

6 slices light sponge cake
little jam
$\frac{1}{4}$ pint ($\frac{2}{3}$ cup) sweet white wine

$\frac{1}{4}$ pint ($\frac{2}{3}$ cup) thick or mixed
thick and thin cream
flaked browned almonds

Spread the cake with jam, put on to the serving dish. Soak with the wine and top with lightly whipped cream and nuts. **Serves 6.**

Apricot Meringue

6 fingers plain cake
4 tablespoons apricot syrup
2 tablespoons apricot brandy

18–24 cooked or canned apricot
halves
2 egg whites
2 oz. ($\frac{1}{4}$ cup) caster sugar
blanched flaked almonds

Put the cake on an oven-proof dish. Blend the syrup and brandy and moisten the cake with this liquid. Arrange apricot halves on top. Whisk the egg whites until very stiff, fold in the sugar. Pile over the fruit, top with the almonds and brown for 3 minutes in a very hot oven. **Serves 6.**

Chocolate Chip Cookies

4 oz. (1 cup) self-raising flour*
3 oz. ($\frac{3}{8}$ cup) luxury margarine
2 oz. ($\frac{1}{4}$ cup) castor sugar

2 oz. plain or cooking chocolate
or special cooking chocolate
'dots'

* Or plain flour sieved with 1 teaspoon baking powder.

Put the flour or flour and baking powder, margarine and sugar into a bowl and cream for about 1 minute. Break the chocolate into small pieces unless using the 'dots'. Blend with the flour mixture. Damp your fingers and roll the mixture into about 12 small balls. Put on to lightly greased baking trays allowing space for them to spread out. Bake for approximately 15 minutes in the centre of a very moderate oven, 325–350°F, Gas Mark 3–4, until pale golden. Cool on the baking trays.
Makes about 12–14.

Crêpes Suzettes

French citrus pancakes

6 oz. (1½ cups) plain flour
pinch salt
2 eggs
¾ pint (2 cups) milk
oil or fat for frying
Filling:
2–3 oz. (¼–⅜ cup) butter
finely grated rind 2 oranges or
   4 tangerines

3 oz. (nearly ¾ cup) icing sugar
little orange or tangerine juice
Sauce:
2 oz. (¼ cup) caster or granulated
   sugar
juice of 2 oranges or 4 tangerines
juice of 1 small lemon
2–3 tablespoons Curaçao or
   Cointreau

Make the pancake batter by beating all the ingredients together. Fry spoonfuls of the batter in a very little hot oil or fat to give about 12 thin pancakes. Blend all the ingredients for the filling together, add just enough fruit juice to give the consistency of thick cream. Put some of the filling into the centre of each cooked pancake, then fold in four.

Put the sugar into a large pan and heat over a low heat until it just begins to turn golden brown. Add the fruit juice and blend with the sugar. Heat the pancakes very gently in the hot sauce. Add the Curaçao or Cointreau just before serving. Ignite if wished.
Serves 6.

Variations:
Although oranges or tangerines are the accepted filling, orange marmalade or red currant jelly could be put into the pancakes. Thin shreds of peel can be soaked, then heated in the sauce with the pancakes.

Although not really part of the classic dish, you can decorate with slices of orange.

Ice Cream Desserts

The large selection of various kinds of ice cream on the market gives splendid scope for menu planning.
Here are quick ideas to use ice cream as the basis for interesting desserts.

Chestnut Sundae

6 tablespoons sweetened
   chestnut purée*
2 tablespoons yoghourt or
   thin cream

4 portions vanilla or
   strawberry ice cream
2 meringue shells**

* From can or tube.
** Ready-prepared variety can be used.

Blend the chestnut purée with the yoghourt or cream. Put the ice cream into glasses, top with the chestnut mixture and coarsely crushed meringues.
Serves 4.

Gondolas

4 portions strawberry ice cream
4 large firm bananas
little apricot jam
squeeze lemon juice

few chopped nuts
few chopped glacé cherries
wafer biscuits

Make sure the ice cream is sufficiently soft to be spread. Peel one strip from each banana – so leaving a boat shape – remove the bananas carefully and mash with the jam and lemon juice. Spoon into the banana cases, top with the ice cream, nuts and cherries. Freeze for a short time then decorate with the biscuits.
Serves 4.

Pineapple Macaroon Sundae

4–6 tablespoons crushed
    pineapple
4 large macaroon biscuits

4 portions vanilla ice cream
4 glacé or Maraschino cherries

Strain any surplus juice from the pineapple. Put the macaroons
on to a serving dish, top with rounds of ice cream and coat
with the pineapple. Decorate with cherries.
Serves 4.

Variations:
Use fairly sharp apple or apricot purée instead of crushed
pineapple.

Praline Fingers

6 tablespoons golden syrup
1 block vanilla ice cream

2–3 tablespoons coarsely chopped
    peanuts or blanched almonds

Boil the syrup until it turns a little darker. Add the nuts.
Put the ice cream on to a serving dish, add the topping.
Serves 4–5.

Party Desserts with Ice Cream

Ice cream can be 'dressed up' for party occasions, for example:
Cut a slice from the top and scoop the pulp from a fresh
pineapple, dice this, mix with Kirsch, pile back again into the
the pineapple case and top with ice cream.
Make the Chestnut Sundae (page 108) more luxurious by adding
a little Tia Maria to the chestnut purée in addition to the
yogourt or cream.
Prepare the Gondolas as page 108 but add Kirsch to the banana
purée.
Melt plain chocolate with a little brandy or strong coffee or
orange juice and spoon over ice cream or pears and ice cream.

Sauces for Ice Cream

Fruit cream sauce:
Blend cold fruit purée with thick cream.

Fudge sauce:
Melt fudge gently with a very little milk.

Jam sauce:
Heat jam with a little fresh lemon or orange juice. Add chopped glacé cherries and nuts if wished.

Peppermint sauce:
Melt plain or chocolate coated peppermint creams in a basin over hot water with a little milk or cream.

Ice Cream Gâteau

The topping on this bought commercial ice cream gives a very imaginative dessert.

Pastry cream topping:
1 oz. ($\frac{1}{4}$ cup) cornflour
$\frac{1}{2}$ pint ($1\frac{1}{4}$ cups) milk
3 oz. ($\frac{3}{8}$ cup) castor sugar
3 egg yolks
$\frac{1}{4}-\frac{1}{2}$ teaspoon vanilla essence
2 oz. ($\frac{1}{3}$ cup) mixed glacé fruits
1 oz. ($\frac{1}{8}$ cup) glacé cherries
Base:
1 block chocolate ice cream

Blend the cornflour and milk, pour into a saucepan. Add the sugar. Cook over a low heat, stirring all the time until the mixture thickens. Remove from the heat, cool slightly, then add the well beaten egg yolks. Transfer to the top of a double saucepan or basin and cook over hot, but not boiling, water for 5–8 minutes to give a thick creamy mixture. Stir in the vanilla essence, cover with damp greaseproof paper and allow to cool. Remove the paper. Add most of the chopped glacé fruits and glacé cherries.
Put the ice cream on to the serving dish and top with the pastry cream and remaining glacé fruits and cherries.
Serves 4–6.

Cream Desserts

A little cream can turn the simplest dessert into a special dish. Use thick cream for a firmer texture or half thick and half thin cream for a lighter sweet. If using two kinds of cream whip the thick type until it holds a shape then gradually whip in thin cream.

Fruit Chiffon

2 teaspoons gelatine
2 tablespoons lemon juice
$\frac{1}{2}$ pint (1$\frac{1}{3}$ cup) sweetened
   thick fruit purée

$\frac{1}{4}$ pint ($\frac{2}{3}$ cup) thick cream
2 egg whites
1 oz. sugar

Soften the gelatine in the cold lemon juice then stand over hot water until dissolved. Stir into the fruit purée. Leave until lightly set then fold in the whipped cream. Whisk the egg whites until very stiff, whisk in the sugar, then fold this meringue mixture into the fruit, etc. Spoon into the glasses. **Serves 4–5.**

Variations:
Use the recipe above as the filling for a flan made from short crust, cornflakes or biscuit crumbs (see page 98).

Banana Cream Syllabub

3 ripe firm bananas
2 tablespoons lemon juice
2 tablespoons white wine

1 oz. sugar
$\frac{1}{2}$ pint (1$\frac{1}{3}$ cup) thick cream

Peel the bananas and mash with the lemon juice, wine and sugar. Whip the cream and fold into the banana mixture. Spoon into serving dishes and chill before serving. **Serves 6.**

112

Jellied Desserts

Although a jelly takes time to set, most jellied desserts are prepared in a very short time. The note at the bottom of the page suggests ways of 'speeding-up' the setting of jellies.

Normandy Mould

1 pint strawberry jelly
$\frac{1}{2}$ pint (1$\frac{1}{3}$ cups) water
$\frac{1}{4}$ pint ($\frac{2}{3}$ cup) apple purée

$\frac{1}{4}$ pint ($\frac{2}{3}$ cup) thin cream
Decoration:
thick cream

Dissolve the jelly in the water. Allow to cool and stiffen slightly then fold in the apple purée then the lightly whipped cream. Spoon into a rinsed mould, allow to set. Turn out and decorate with cream.
Serves 4–6.

Variation:
Spanish mould: Use a lemon jelly and apricot purée together with 2–3 tablespoons finely chopped blanched almonds.

To save time:
Dissolve the jelly in the minimum quantity of very hot water. Crush enough ice to make up the full quantity of liquid. Stir into the very hot jelly and it will set within minutes.
Another method of 'speeding-up' the setting of the jelly is to dissolve it in the minimum of very hot water, then to add cold water to give correct quantity. Stand the cold jelly in a bowl surrounded by ice cubes or put into the freezing compartment or freezer for a short time until it begins to set.

Mandarin Whip

small can Mandarin oranges
1 pint orange jelly

2 eggs
1 oz. sugar

Drain the syrup from the canned oranges, pour into a measure and add enough water to give just under $\frac{3}{4}$ pint (2 cups). Heat and dissolve the jelly in this, whisk on to the beaten egg yolks while still warm. Allow to set lightly. Whisk the egg whites until very stiff, gradually whisk in the sugar. Fold the chopped orange segments and then the meringue mixture into the lightly set jelly. Spoon into dishes or a serving bowl. Serves 4–6.

Variations:
Pineapple whip: Use lemon jelly and diced pineapple rings or crushed pineapple.
Soft fruit whip: Use raspberry or strawberry jelly and uncooked berry fruit. This means using all water to dissolve the jelly.

Caramel Jelly

Caramel:
4 oz. ($\frac{1}{2}$ cup) sugar (loaf or granulated)
4 tablespoons water

Jelly mixture:
$\frac{3}{4}$ pint (2 cups) water
$\frac{1}{2}$ oz. gelatine
squeeze lemon juice

Stir the sugar and water over the heat in a strong saucepan until the sugar dissolves. Boil, without stirring, until golden brown caramel. Add about 3 tablespoons cold water from the $\frac{3}{4}$ pint (2 cups) and stir until blended with the caramel. Keep this warm. Soften the gelatine in 2 tablespoons cold water from the remaining water. Add to the caramel mixture then stir until dissolved. Pour into the remainder of the cold water, add the lemon juice and allow to set. Serve with cream or ice cream. Serves 4–6.

Cakes and Cookies

The following recipe needs no cooking, it is made and left to set.

No-Cook Chocolate Cake

4 oz. plain or cooking chocolate
4 oz. ($\frac{1}{2}$ cup) butter or margarine
4 oz. ($\frac{2}{3}$ cup) golden syrup

4 oz. (generous $\frac{1}{2}$ cup) sultanas
2 oz. ($\frac{1}{3}$ cup) glacé cherries
$7\frac{1}{2}$ oz. semi-sweet biscuits

Put the chocolate, butter or margarine and syrup into a large saucepan. Heat just until a smooth mixture. Add the sultanas and the quartered cherries while the mixture is still warm, then allow this to cool. Crush the biscuits into fairly fine crumbs, either in the liquidizer or between two sheets of greaseproof paper (using a rolling pin). Tip the biscuit crumbs into the chocolate mixture and mix well. Line a loaf tin with greaseproof paper and put in the biscuit mixture. Press down firmly and allow to set. It takes at least 30 minutes in the refrigerator.
Makes about 10–12 slices.

Variations:
Add a few chopped nuts to the mixture.
Cover the cake with icing made by melting about 4 oz. plain or cooking chocolate with 2 oz. ($\frac{1}{4}$ cup) butter and then allowing this to cool and blending in 4 oz. (nearly 1 cup) sieved icing sugar.

To save time:
Put into the home freezer or freezing compartment of the refrigerator for approximately 10–15 minutes to solidify. These cakes can be made well ahead and stored in the refrigerator for some weeks.

116

Coconut Pyramids

large can full cream sweetened
  condensed milk
few drops colouring

about 9 oz. (3 cups) desiccated
  coconut
rice paper

Mix the milk and enough coconut to make a fairly firm consistency. Colour some of the mixture pale pink, pale green, etc. Form into pyramid shapes and put on to rice paper. Although the mixture may be left to harden with exposure to the air, it can be put into the oven to brown. Lift carefully on to ungreased baking trays and leave for about 10 minutes only in the centre of a very moderate oven, 325–350°F, Gas Mark 3–4, until golden brown. Cool, then cut round the rice paper.

Makes about 16.

Note: If rice paper is not available then put on to lightly greased baking trays if putting these in the oven. If allowing to set, leave on a metal tray – do not grease this. Coconut pyramids should be left for several hours to harden if you do not intend browning the mixture.

Variations:

Add a little chocolate powder or instant coffee to the condensed milk before adding the coconut.

Tutti frutti bars: Recipe as above, but use slightly less desiccated coconut. Add about 4 oz. (1 cup) finely chopped nuts (any kind), 4 oz. (generous $\frac{1}{2}$ cup) chopped raisins, 2 oz. ($\frac{1}{2}$ cup) chopped glacé cherries. Put one sheet of rice paper into a 6–7-inch shallow tin. Add the mixture, then cover with rice paper and a light weight. Leave for 24 hours, and cut into squares.

To make more economical tutti frutti bars:

Add 4 oz. (1 cup) soft cake or biscuit crumbs to the condensed milk, then as much desiccated coconut as needed to make a fairly firm mixture. Add some or all of the ingredients suggested in the recipe above. Both this and recipe above make about 24 squares.

Speedy Gâteaux

Ready-made plain cakes can be turned into special gâteaux by making interesting fillings and toppings (see recipes that follow).
Cake mixes and the modern methods of mixing (as typified below) enable cakes to be made easily and speedily.
When using the modern quick mixing fat, margarine or oil, it is important to increase the raising agent to compensate for the short creaming time.

Austrian Chocolate Gâteau

3 tablespoons milk
1 level teaspoon cocoa
2 oz. plain or cooking chocolate
5 oz. ($1\frac{1}{4}$ cups) self-raising flour*
1 teaspoon baking powder*

5 oz. ($\frac{5}{8}$ cup) castor sugar
5 oz. ($\frac{5}{8}$ cup) luxury margarine
2 large eggs
Filling and icing:
apricot jam
whipped cream
4 oz. plain or cooking chocolate

* Or plain flour with $2\frac{1}{2}$ teaspoons baking powder.

Heat the milk, then add the cocoa and chocolate (broken into pieces) and stir until dissolved. Cool slightly. Sieve the flour and baking powder into a bowl. Add the sugar, margarine and eggs and cream for 1 minute, then gradually stir in the milk mixture.
Grease and flour two 7–8-inch sandwich tins. Divide the mixture between these. Bake above the centre of a very moderate to moderate oven, 325–375°F, Gas Mark 4–5, until firm to the touch; this takes approximately 20–25 minutes. Turn out and cool. Sandwich with apricot jam and whipped cream. Top with apricot jam then a thick layer of melted chocolate.
Makes about 8–9 slices.

Peach Gâteau

5 tablespoons oil*
3 eggs
$1\frac{1}{4}$ tablespoons water
6 oz. ($1\frac{1}{2}$ cups) self-raising flour**
1 teaspoon baking powder**

6 oz. ($\frac{3}{4}$ cup) castor sugar
$\frac{1}{4}-\frac{1}{2}$ pint ($\frac{2}{3}-1\frac{1}{3}$ cups) whipped cream
small to medium can sliced peaches
sieved icing sugar

* Do not use olive oil, but one of the light oils made specially for all kinds of cooking.
** Or plain flour and $2\frac{1}{2}$ level teaspoons baking powder.

Whisk the oil, egg yolks and water until the mixture forms an opaque thick mixture. This stage is very important. Sieve the flour and baking powder, mix with the sugar and stir into the egg yolk mixture, beat well. Whisk the egg whites until very stiff, then fold into the oil mixture.

Put into two 7-inch greased and floured sandwich tins and bake as the recipe for Vanilla Layer Gâteau, overleaf. Turn out and cool.

Sandwich together with whipped cream and well drained peaches. Top with sieved icing sugar or with more cream and peaches.

Makes 6–8 slices.

Note: The recipe above makes a sponge that keeps well. For a lighter sponge reduce the amount of oil to 3 tablespoons only and use $3\frac{1}{2}$ tablespoons water or other liquid. The above is a basic method of using oil rather than other fats in a cake. It is not only quick to use but it is ideal for people who wish to avoid other types of fat.

Variations:

Coffee sponge: Omit the water and use sweetened coffee essence or very strong coffee instead.

Fruit sponges: Add a little grated lemon or orange rind to the oil and egg yolks and use fruit juice in place of water.

Vanilla Layer Gâteau

Cake:
6 oz. (1½ cups) self-raising flour*
1 teaspoon baking powder*
3½ oz. (just under ½ cup) white fat
4 oz. (½ cup) castor sugar
2 large eggs
4½ tablespoons milk
¼ teaspoon vanilla essence

Filling and icing:
8 oz. (2 cups) sieved icing sugar
4 oz. (½ cup) white fat
2 tablespoons milk
¼–½ teaspoon vanilla essence
Decoration:
few glacé cherries
little angelica

* Or plain flour with 2¼ teaspoons baking powder.

Put all the ingredients for the cake into a large bowl and stir gently for about 1 minute, then beat well with a wooden spoon until blended. Divide between two 6–7-inch greased and floured sandwich tins and bake for approximately 20 minutes above the centre of a very moderate to moderate oven, 350–375°F, Gas Mark 4–5. Turn out carefully and cool. Sandwich together and top with the icing made by putting all the ingredients into a bowl and beating until smooth. Decorate with halved cherries and angelica.
Makes 6–8 slices.

Variations:
Lemon or orange gâteau: Omit the vanilla essence and blend both the cake and the icing with fruit juice instead of milk. A little very finely grated lemon or orange rind may be added too.
Coffee gâteau: Use strong coffee in place of milk in both the cake and the icing.
Cup cakes: Divide the cake mixture between about 18 paper cases. Bake for 10–12 minutes towards the top of a moderately hot oven. Top with icing.

To save time:
Use the electric mixer on medium speed for about 1 minute only.

YOGURT WHIP *(Photograph: Eden Vale Ltd.)*

Using Yogourt

Yogourt is one of the interesting developments of modern times which has its origin in an old traditional method of treating milk. Today it is possible to produce yogourt itself at home or to buy a great variety of different flavours.

Serve natural yogourt (often spelt yogurt or yoghurt) by itself or flavoured with cinnamon or nutmeg or serve it with cooked or dessert fruits. It makes an excellent low-calorie dessert.

Add yogourt to a half set jelly – allow only about $\frac{3}{4}$ pint (2 cups) water to make the jelly, then stir in $\frac{1}{4}$ pint ($\frac{2}{3}$ cup) natural or fruit flavoured yogourt.

Use yogourt in place of ice cream in a sundae with layers of jelly and fruit to give interest.

A fruit fool can be made in the same way as the recipe below, but omit the egg white.

Yogourt Whip

approximately $\frac{1}{2}$ pint ($1\frac{1}{3}$ cups) thick sweetened fruit purée
$\frac{1}{4}$ pint ($\frac{2}{3}$ cup) natural yogourt

1 egg white
Decoration:
fruit

The purée can be obtained in various ways. If using ripe strawberries or other soft fruit just mash, sieve or emulsify and add sugar to taste. Hard fruit should be cooked in the minimum of water (or omit water if possible) with sugar to taste, then mashed, sieved or emulsified. If using canned or defrosted frozen fruit, strain off the syrup (this can be used in a fruit salad or jelly), mash, sieve or emulsify. Add extra sugar if required.

Chill the yogourt well then beat into the cold purée. Add the stiffly whisked egg white. Spoon into glasses, decorate with fruit and serve at once. The mixture tends to separate if left standing.

Serves 3–4.

Snacks

One of the quickest ways to provide a hot snack is to put food on toasted bread. The following are some of the very speedy (and nutritious) snacks that can be served within minutes.
All quantities are enough for 2 small or 4 large pieces of toast. If butter (or margarine) is among the ingredients in the spread there is no need to butter the toast.

Devilled ham:
Chop 4 oz. ham finely, then blend with 2 oz. ($\frac{1}{4}$ cup) butter or margarine, 1 teaspoon curry powder, 1 tablespoon finely chopped chutney and a few drops of Worcestershire sauce. Add a shake of cayenne pepper too if wished. Spread on the hot toast and heat for a few minutes. (Canned ham is excellent in this recipe).

Devilled Tongue:
Use cooked tongue instead of ham.

Ham and tomatoes:
Put slices of ham on buttered toast, top with sliced tomatoes and seasoning. Heat for a few minutes.

Creamed salmon:
Blend flaked salmon with a very little mayonnaise and top of the milk or thin cream. Season well and flavour with a few capers and chopped gherkins. Spread on the buttered toast and heat gently.

Sardines on toast:
Mash the sardines with a little lemon juice and seasoning. Spread over the buttered toast and heat. The fish may be topped with grated cheese before heating if wished.

Toasted cheese:
Spread buttered toast with fairly thick slices of Gruyère, Cheddar, Dutch or other cooking cheese. Heat for a few minutes under the grill.

Following page: TOASTED CHEESE

Welsh Rarebit

1 oz. butter or margarine
1 teaspoon made mustard
seasoning (including shake of
  cayenne pepper)

1 tablespoon beer or milk
6 oz. (1½ cups) grated Cheddar
  cheese
4 slices buttered toast

Blend the butter or margarine, mustard, seasoning, beer or milk and cheese well. Spread over the hot buttered toast and brown under the grill.
Serves 4.

Crab and Tomato Toasts

4 small rounds bread
2 oz. (¼ cup) butter
½ lemon
small crab or can crabmeat
seasoning

2 tablespoons fresh or
  1 tablespoon concentrated
  tomato purée
Garnish:
½–1 lemon
watercress or lettuce

Toast the bread, spread with half the butter. Squeeze the juice from the ½ lemon, blend with the flaked crabmeat, the tomato purée and the rest of the butter. Season well and spread on to the hot toast. Heat for a few minutes, then serve hot garnished with lemon and watercress or lettuce.
Serves 4.

Mock Crab

1 oz. butter or margarine
3 eggs
seasoning

few drops anchovy essence
2–3 tablespoons very finely
  grated cheese
2–3 slices buttered toast

Heat the butter or margarine in a pan, add the beaten eggs, seasoning and anchovy essence and scramble very lightly. Stir in the cheese and serve on toast.
Serves 2–3.

This is also excellent cold for salads or sandwich fillings.

Preceding page: CRAB AND TOMATO TOASTS

Index